THE GOLDEN GARDEN BLUEPRINT

Building Extraordinary Wealth in the Digital Era

By Jenny Connolley

Investor • Educator • Intuitive

Founder: Intuitive Wealth Academy

The Golden Garden Blueprint

Building Extraordinary Wealth in the Digital Era

Cover Designed by Jenny Connolley and Kimberly Olson

www.JennyConnolley.com

ISBN 979-8-9968688-7-2

For every woman who's ready to break the cycle.

May this book awaken the investor within you.

May it ignite the courage to dream bigger, earn bigger, build bigger, give bigger, live bigger and love bigger than ever imagined.

May you plant seeds that grow into freedom, abundance, prosperity and a legacy that blesses generations.

You are the Chosen One.

Acknowledgements

To everything, my number one, my biggest fan, my protector, my best friend, my adventure partner, my lover, and my world, My Honey-**Tom Connolley**.

From our very first date, we've been together! Nearly 20 years of loving you from the first kiss. Thank you for loving every ounce of me and my imperfections. Thank you for giving me the freedom to dream as big as my heart desires. Thank you for letting me fly wildly, boldly, without restraints, and slightly recklessly. Thank you for forgiving me. Thank you for always keeping me laughing and standing beside me through every season of life's greatness and defeat. Your sexy blue eyes captivate my heart over and over, every day! With you, I am home, I am safe, and I am adored! I'm the luckiest girl in the world, being married to YOU. I love you more than the last number times infinity.

To all of my Light-Leading Soul Sisters, my soul family—**Rosemary, Mercedes, Tracy, Krista, Taylor & My Family Lindsey, Jillian,** and my sister, **Melissa Mobley**. Plus the many more unmentioned: Thank you for your endless uplifting encouragement, for praying with me, for celebrating with me, for speaking truth into my life, and for reminding me of who I am whenever I needed it most. Your light has brightened my life in ways you may never fully understand, and I will forever be grateful for the gift of your friendship.

Special shoutout to **Mercedes Davis,** my SoulFire Flame, who walked diligently by my side, day after day, during our "Writers Window," where we dedicated undisturbed time to completing this book. Without you, this book would still be in my head as only a thought of, "One day I'll write that book." With you, I can move mountains. My Mount Everest!

To my mentors, **Linda P. Jones and Kimberly Olson**, thank you for helping shape this journey. Both of you entered my life at the same time. Thank you, GOD!

Linda, thank you for opening my eyes to a completely different way of understanding wealth, investing, and financial stewardship. Your wisdom gave me the confidence to become the avid investor God designed me to be.

Kimberly, thank you for being a beautiful example of leadership, integrity, and service. You have inspired me since the very beginning of my entrepreneurial journey, and today, I am deeply honored to call you my coach, my publisher, and my friend.

To my **Mom and Dad** in Heaven, thank you for giving me life and for loving me unconditionally. I am grateful for every memory we shared and every lesson you taught me. Although our relationship looks different today, I feel your presence with me every second of every day. I know you are still walking beside me, celebrating every milestone, cheering me on from Heaven, and reminding me that love never ends. I love you, and I carry you with me always.

To my father-like best friend, **Mike Millar**, thank you for stepping into my life when my heart needed it most. After losing my dad, you filled a space that felt impossible to fill. Your belief in me, your admiration for my dreams, your constant encouragement, and your unwavering support over the past eleven years have meant more than words could ever express. I am forever grateful for our friendship, and I smile knowing you are reunited with God, my mom and my dad. Until we meet again, my Hot Rocket!

To My Dearest **Guzman family**, thank you for giving me the beautiful gift of becoming a bonus mom and grandmother. I am so very proud of each of you. Know that you are loved, unconditionally, always.

As I look around, I realize how incredibly blessed I am. I have extraordinary Light Leaders walking beside me here on Earth and an incredible team of angels surrounding me in Heaven. I am held by love, guided by faith, and strengthened by the unwavering support of those seen and unseen. My heart overflows with gratitude for every soul who has walked this journey with me.

It's go time.

Let's change the world together.

A Special Gift from Jenny

Your Complimentary Wealth Activation

Thank you for choosing this book.

The fact that you're holding these pages tells me something about you.

You believe your future can be greater than your past.

You know you're here for more.

And you're ready to cultivate a life of wealth, freedom, and legacy.

Before you turn the page, I'd love to give you a special gift.

I've created a complimentary **Wealth Activation** to help prepare your heart, renew your mind, and awaken the investor within you before you begin this journey.

This guided experience will help you release old money stories, expand your vision, and step into the woman who confidently creates lasting wealth.

I encourage you to listen to it before you begin reading, then return to it whenever you need a reminder of who you're becoming.

Simply scan the QR code or visit:

JennyConnolley.com/GoldenGardenBlueprint

I'm so honored you're here.

Now...

Let's plant the first seed.

With love,

Jenny Connolley

"Every extraordinary harvest begins with a single seed."

Before We Begin

Important Disclaimer

This book is provided for educational, informational, and inspirational purposes only. Nothing contained in these pages should be interpreted as financial, investment, legal, or other professional advice. I am not a licensed financial advisor, investment advisor, attorney, CPA, tax professional, or fiduciary.

I hold a degree in finance and have been investing for more than 25 years, including in cryptocurrency since 2017. Everything shared in this book is based on my personal experiences, research, opinions, and lessons learned throughout my journey.

Any references to investing, cryptocurrency, digital assets, business strategies, wealth-building principles, or financial decisions are provided solely for educational purposes. They are not guarantees, endorsements, or promises of future performance or financial results–ONLY MAYBE'S AND WHAT IF'S.

All investing involves risk. Cryptocurrency and digital assets are especially highly volatile, and you could lose part or all of your investment. Past performance is never a guarantee of future results.

Always conduct your own research, use your intuition and seek advice from qualified professionals before making decisions that may affect your finances or your future.

By reading this book, you acknowledge that you are solely responsible for your own decisions, actions, investments, and results. Neither I nor any of my companies, employees, contractors, or affiliates shall be liable for any loss, damages, or consequences arising from the use of the information contained in this book.

My hope is that these pages inspire you to think differently, pursue wisdom, strengthen your wealth consciousness, and become a faithful steward of the opportunities God has placed before you.

CONTENTS

Foreword

Jenny Connolley has a gift for making the possibilities of wealth-building feel both accessible and inspiring. Through her thoughtful insights, practical investing ideas, and encouraging guidance, she invites women to envision a future where growing their wealth is not only possible but achievable. The knowledge shared in these pages has the potential to change lives—not simply by increasing financial resources, but by expanding what's possible for the future.

Jenny approaches life with genuine enthusiasm, curiosity, and generosity. She has a passion for learning, growing, and helping others do the same. To know Jenny is truly a joy.

It has been my privilege to serve as Jenny's wealth mentor over the years and to watch her develop both the confidence and knowledge to become an educator in her own right. Seeing her share what she has learned with others is incredibly rewarding.

My hope is that this book inspires you to plant the seeds of your own financial future. As you cultivate your knowledge and take purposeful action, you'll discover that wealth—like

Jenny's golden garden—grows with patience, care, and consistent attention.

Jenny has created a wonderful guide to help you begin that journey. I hope you enjoy it as much as I have.

Linda P. Jones

America's Wealth Mentor, www.LindaPJones.com

Introduction

It's Time to Wake Up My Ladies...*(And men, if you're here, welcome too.)*

The Wealth Wave Is Here.

Okay, friends... welcome.

I am so glad you're here.

Let me be real with you right from the start. It took me a very long time to come public with this information. I'm really hard on myself and I have a challenging time sharing my wisdom. During the writing of this book, there were many moments I wanted to quit and throw the whole thing in the trash. Yet here it is, in your hands, by the grace of God.

I made the decision to finish because I KNOW, not believe, I know what I'm sharing has the ability to dramatically change the financial future of those who are willing to learn with an open mind. What you're receiving is my passionate heart, years of investing, study, mentorship, research, prayer, and bold action. It is the wise counsel that has found me through experience, and I know for certain this book is 100% Spirit-led.

One thing you should know about me is that I'm radically optimistic. In my Vedic birth chart, Jupiter is placed in my first house, so it's natural for me to see possibilities where others see obstacles. Jupiter is also retrograde, which brings delay in confidence of teaching and delay in abundance. That all changes now! I spent many years quietly studying, learning, preparing, and growing before ever stepping into teaching. Looking back, I can clearly see that God was preparing me long before He called me to educate, lead, and serve as a Light Leader.

I've learned to release timelines and trust God's timing. I go all in. I play all out. I'm fiercely committed to the bigger picture and the soul mission I know I was created to fulfill. My conviction is unshakable. My faith reaches beyond concepts because it has been built through experience.

Some of my decisions probably look insane to the average person. Some of them are!

I'm perfectly okay with that.

I trust God first. I am deeply supported by my parents, who continue walking beside me from Heaven. I am connected to my guardian angels, my spirit guides, my ancestors, and my own inner knowing, my intuition also known as the Holy

Spirit. Every decision I make is filtered through prayer, discernment, research, wisdom, and trust.

I encourage you to do the same.

I am simply sharing my experiences, my opinions, and what I have learned along the way.

Trust your intuition.

Do your own research.

Make the decisions that feel right for you.

My goal is to open the door to what I know in my heart is one of the greatest financial opportunities of our lifetime. Once you feel that same conviction, move forward fearlessly.

Our financial economy is changing at the speed of light. The systems we've been using for decades are outdated, slow, and expensive, while the technology surrounding us has advanced faster than anyone could have imagined. We've already embraced a digital world. It's already here. We tap our credit cards, send money through Venmo, Zelle, and PayPal, and manage our finances from the palm of our hand. Press some buttons and packages arrive at your doorstep.

The financial system is simply catching up to the way we already live.

The laws are being written.

The infrastructure is being built.

Those who choose courage over comfort, who are willing to take the risk, and who invest in this global shift will be rewarded.

Blockchain technology will become as common as sending a text message or an email. Just as very few people had ever heard of Venmo, Zelle, or PayPal fifteen years ago, digital assets and blockchain technology are quietly becoming the next evolution of money.

Many millionaires and billionaires will be created during this financial transformation because they recognized the opportunity while it was unfolding.

My desire is for you to become one of them.

This transformation is happening whether you're investing or not. My mission is to create more women investors than ever before because I know what happens when resources are placed into the hands of women with beautiful hearts and powerful Soul-Led Missions.

I have a finance degree and have been an avid investor for more than twenty-five years, including investing in cryptocurrency since 2017. I've spent years learning from some of the brightest financial minds and wealth mentors in the world. My favorite of them all was kind enough to write the foreword for this book, Linda P. Jones.

I've walked through the confusion, made the mistakes, spent countless hours researching, and blazed through the fire so you can enter **The Golden Garden Blueprint** with greater clarity, confidence, and peace of mind.

My mission is to bring this knowledge to the forefront of as many women, families, and future Light Leaders as possible. The world needs more people who care deeply about their communities, their children, their animals, the environment, and leaving this world better than they found it.

The more money we have, the more freedom we have. The more freedom we have, the more stress lifts from our shoulders. The bigger the stages we stand on, the more we can pour into communities we love, the more lives we impact.

Money is a resource.

Resources create choices.

Choices create freedom.

Freedom gives us the opportunity to answer the calling God placed on our hearts.

Imagine what could happen if thousands of Light Leaders became extraordinarily wealthy and abundant. Imagine the difference we could make together.

Everything changes when your purpose shifts from *"I need to earn more money"* to *"How can I use my wealth to serve?"*

Imagine the businesses we could build, the families we could bless, the children we could educate, the charities we could fund, the communities we could strengthen, and the countless lives we could change.

When wealth is guided by purpose, it becomes one of the greatest forces for good in the world.

This journey has never been just about building financial freedom. It has always been about becoming a wise steward of the resources entrusted to you, using them to create a legacy that extends far beyond your own lifetime.

That is the heart of **The Golden Garden Blueprint**.

This philosophy is exactly how I've designed this book.

This book is organized into four parts, following what I call **The 4P Method™**:

Prepare. Plant. Protect. Prosper.

Every thriving garden follows this same rhythm. First, we prepare the soil. Then we plant the seeds. We faithfully protect what we've planted, and in time, we prosper from the harvest.

Building extraordinary wealth follows that very same path.

I encourage you to read this book from beginning to end the first time through because each chapter prepares you for the next season of your journey. Then come back to it often. Highlight it, write in the margins, complete the exercises, and allow it to become your personal blueprint as you continue building your Golden Garden.

By the time you reach the final page, you'll have far more than knowledge. You'll have a clear vision, a practical framework, powerful tools, and the confidence to navigate one of the greatest wealth transfers in modern history with wisdom, conviction, and purpose.

Looking back, I can honestly say every season of my procrastination, all of my overthinking, every delay happened in divine timing. This book was never meant to arrive a year ago. It was meant to arrive now. TODAY!

We are standing on the front edge of one of the greatest financial transformations the world has ever experienced. A massive wave of change has already begun building momentum, and over the next several years we'll watch history unfold in real time as entire industries evolve, the way money moves transforms, new opportunities emerge, new leaders rise, and families create generational wealth through preparation, education, and courageous action.

One of my favorite sayings is, **Build as You Fly.**

Every leap of faith I've taken happened well before I felt completely ready. Clarity arrives through movement. Wisdom has come through experience. Confidence has been built by taking action.

I'll leave you with one question.

When history looks back on this extraordinary season, will you remember watching it happen, or will you remember becoming part of it?

Welcome to **The Golden Garden Blueprint.**

The soil is waiting.

Let's begin.

PART I

PREPARE

PART I: PREPARE

Wisdom from Proverbs

"I went past the field of a sluggard, past the vineyard of someone who had no sense; thorns had come up everywhere, the ground was covered with weeds, and the stone wall was in ruins."

— Proverbs 24:30–31

At first glance, it looked like a worthless piece of land.

The field was covered in weeds. Thorns stretched in every direction, and the stone wall that once protected it had fallen into disrepair.

Most people would have walked away believing the land had no future.

The writer of Proverbs saw something different.

He recognized that the problem wasn't the soil.

The problem was neglect.

The field still possessed everything it needed to produce an abundant harvest. It simply required someone willing to clear the weeds, rebuild the walls, and prepare the ground.

The same is true of our financial lives.

Many people believe they aren't capable of building wealth. They blame their upbringing, their income, their past mistakes, or the economy. Yet beneath every limiting belief lies incredible potential waiting to be uncovered.

Your financial future isn't determined by where you begin.

It's determined by what you're willing to cultivate.

Before you can plant the seeds of wealth, you must first prepare the soil.

That's exactly what this first part of the book is about.

Together, we'll pull the weeds of fear, doubt, and misinformation. We'll rebuild a strong financial foundation. We'll prepare the ground so that when it's time to invest, your seeds have every opportunity to flourish.

Because healthy soil always produces a better harvest.

CHAPTER 1

Prepare the Soil

"Out of suffering have emerged the strongest souls; the most massive characters are seared with scars."

— Khalil Gibran

Release. Cleanse. Purify.

My clearing of the soil began when my husband and I left Lake Tahoe, CA for Dallas, TX. Stepping into the unknown, bigger than any time in the past. This was NEW BEGINNINGS for our Marriage, our Career, our Lives.

We spent the first three years of our relationship chasing adventure, packing up every six months to explore somewhere new. Every road trip became another chapter of our story. Tom was always behind the wheel, and I happily claimed my role as co-pilot. We laughed, dreamed, and planted seeds of a life we couldn't wait to build together.

Ten years later, after putting down roots in beautiful Lake Tahoe, CA, we purchased our first home. It felt like everything we had worked toward was finally coming together. From the outside, life looked picture perfect.

Behind closed doors, however, I was fighting battles I didn't know how to face. After the traumatic loss of my father, followed by the deaths of my grandfather and uncle, I found myself reaching for alcohol as a way to numb the grief I wasn't allowing myself to feel. What began as a coping mechanism slowly became a form of self-sabotage, quietly eroding the very life we had worked so hard to create.

Our dear friend, Matt Timcho, presented us with an opportunity to move to Texas and sell roofs.

What did I know about roofs? Nothing.

What did I know about entrepreneurship? Nothing.

Apparently, you door knock to find business? Again, something I knew absolutely nothing about.

So we jumped!

Knowing our love was undeniably unbreakable, off we went, putting a "For Sale" sign on the first gem of real estate we had purchased and setting sail for new beginnings with the faith that together we could accomplish EVERYTHING. Spoiler Alert- WE DID!

Even though I'd been across the country several times during our years of "nomadic life-The Nomads," as my mother called us, this was my first time driving by myself with my two kitties. So you know what that means... I got to listen to exactly what I wanted. YAY!

That's when I discovered the **Be Wealthy and Smart** podcast by Linda P. Jones. I binge-listened to every episode from California to Texas. Her podcasts captivated me, delivering power-packed information on the stock market, the economy, market trends, tax tips, and building wealth. I could feel my confidence as an entrepreneur growing exponentially.

Then something happened.

She started talking about cryptocurrency...

More on that later.

Unlearn. Forgive. Return.

Clearing the land means purging and unlearning the toxic habits, beliefs, and conditioning you've carried from the past. It is an unveiling. It's a process, and at times, a bit of a bitch.

You gradually return to who you were before the world told you who to be. No one else can do this work for you. It's the hardest and most rewarding thing you'll ever do for yourself.

This is the Work you hear awakened people speak about.

I had a lot of work to do in this area, and the first step was learning to forgive myself. As painful as it is to admit, that took years.

Surprisingly, as we settled in and learned everything we could about roofing, I still felt the itch for something more. A friend introduced me to an MLM (multi-level marketing) business, and WOW... that was a game changer for me.

The real transformation came from the mindset training.

Entrepreneurs from all backgrounds openly and freely shared how to clear the garage in our minds, dream boldly, and think bigger. There were meetings almost every day and endless lists of books to read. Looking back, 2017 was the year I truly started discovering who I was.

During that time, I found Kimberly Olson. She created incredible videos on how to build a business using social media, and I applied everything I learned to help grow our roofing company. Fast forward to today, and she's my personal coach and publisher.

Amazing how life comes full circle.

Side note: If you're just beginning your personal development or spiritual journey, joining a network marketing company can be one of the most affordable ways to accelerate your growth. Looking back, I realize I received coaching, mentorship, and leadership training that would cost me thousands of dollars to access today. At the time, I received much of it simply by showing up, learning, and being part of the community.

If you're looking for someone who teaches this space with integrity and excellence, I highly recommend my coach, publisher and friend, Kimberly Olson. She has helped thousands of entrepreneurs build businesses while developing the mindset and leadership skills that create lasting success. Tell her I sent you!

Tom and I found our footing in the roofing industry much faster than either of us imagined. Within just six months, we had become top sales producers and generated more than $1 million in roof sales.

Then life reminded us, once again, how quickly everything can change.

The bell of loss rang again, this time calling Tom's beloved mother home.

Losing her shook him to his core. Tom was an only child, raised by his mother, and they shared a bond few people ever experience. She wasn't just his mom. She was his best friend, his biggest supporter, and his most loyal companion. Tom has always been someone who carries his pain quietly. Instead of expressing it outwardly, he carried it deep within.

Only nine days after saying goodbye to his mom, Tom suffered a sudden medical crisis that came out of nowhere. One moment he was healthy. The next, he was fighting for his life in the ICU, on a ventilator, while family and friends prayed without ceasing.

I had barely begun grieving the loss of his mother. Now I was sitting beside the man I loved, wondering if I was about to lose him too.

Then, a miracle unfolded.

A surgeon who wasn't even scheduled to be there answered the call. Faced with an extraordinarily high-risk procedure that had never been performed in that exact way before, he chose to try. Against all odds, the surgery was a success.

On the Fourth of July, as fireworks lit up the New York City skyline, Tom opened his eyes.

After nearly two weeks in the hospital, he finally came home.

Walking so closely with death changed us. Our love grew deeper than ever before. We stopped taking ordinary moments for granted. Every sunrise, every conversation, every embrace became a gift.

Looking back, I couldn't understand why we kept walking through so much grief. I questioned God. I searched for meaning.

Today, I see the message with complete clarity.

Life is precious. Life is fragile. None of us are promised tomorrow.

Chase the dream. Build the business. Buy the ticket. Take the trip. Tell people you love them. Forgive quickly. Release yesterday. Release regret. Release judgment. Release fear.

Live fully. Love deeply. Give generously. Become everything you were created to become while you still have the opportunity.

A few months later, our friend Matt Timcho looked at us and said, "Y'all ready yet? Let's start our own roofing business!"

In typical Jenny form, I said I wasn't ready. I needed more experience. I didn't know what I was doing. I needed more research.

So we went to work for a competitor, someone I thought had it all figured out. They had the big teams, the trucks, the marketing. From the outside, everything looked successful.

It didn't take long to realize we knew enough.

A few months later, I finally got over my fears and said, "Let's do it!"

In 2018, TC Roofing & Restorations was born.

We had grit, determination, and unwavering faith, so onward we went. We built our business with a passion to serve and a commitment to bringing integrity and a positive reputation to the roofing industry.

Then another wave appeared on the horizon.

We were about a year and a half into building our business. I had been testing the waters of sobriety and self-love, yet I was still caught up in hustle culture.

Then, I'll be damned...

God came for my mother.

On January 8, 2020, she was called home.

Just like my father, she left this world without sickness, without warning, and without any indication her time had come. One day she was here. The next, she was gone.

After watching Tom's mother spend several months in the hospital, I can now look at the way my parents' passed as a blessing. Even though we never got the chance to say formal goodbyes, neither of them suffered, and neither saw it coming.

Fear consumed my body in a way I could never fully put into words. After my mom passed, I was in complete shock, paralyzed by fear.

I knew I couldn't allow self-sabotage, depression, and numbing to consume me the way they had after my dad passed on April 8, 2015. I also knew this mountain would be bigger than any I had ever climbed.

This time, I refused to sink.

I had no idea how I was going to rise above it, only that I had to.

So I dove headfirst into every healing modality I could find.

That's when a friend introduced me to breathwork.

Not pranayama breathing. This was deep, transformational, three-part conscious connected breathing that could unlock years of stored emotion in just 30 to 45 minutes.

It changed my life.

For the first time, I could feel the soil beginning to soften. Years of buried pain, grief, fear, and self-sabotage finally began to give way to healing.

This was the purification my soul needed. It became the bridge back to the woman God had created me to be.

If you've never experienced transformational breathwork, I encourage you to. It has the power to reconnect you with parts of yourself you may have forgotten were there. If you'd like to experience one of my guided breathwork journeys, visit www.JennyConnolley.com.

CHAPTER 2

Pull the Weeds

"Whether you think you can, or you think you can't—you're right."

— Henry Ford

Awareness: What are we starting with?

Avoidance allows weeds to spread. Awareness allows gardens to grow.

There are other weeds we rarely talk about.

What if I lose the money?
What if I make the wrong investment?
What if I become successful and people judge me?
What if I have more money than anyone in my family has ever had?
What if money comes easily? Do I even deserve it?

These quiet questions often shape our financial lives more than we realize.

Many of us were taught that the only way to earn more money is to work harder. We trade our time for a paycheck, believing it's the only path to financial freedom.

One of the most transformative shifts you can make is moving from working for money to allowing your money to work for you.

As the saying goes, *"Compound interest is the eighth wonder of the world. He who understands it, earns it. He who doesn't, pays it."*

Whether or not those exact words came from Albert Einstein, the principle is undeniable.

Compounding is one of the greatest wealth-building forces on the planet.

Every dollar you save and invest has the potential to earn more dollars, which then earn even more dollars. Over time, your wealth begins creating more wealth.

Think about some of the wealthiest people in the world. They didn't build extraordinary wealth by earning bigger paychecks alone. They built businesses, owned real estate, invested in companies, and accumulated appreciating assets.

Their money continued growing long after the initial work had been done.

That is one of the greatest financial shifts you will ever make.

Extraordinary wealth is rarely created by working harder. It's built through faithful stewardship, consistent investing, ownership, patience, and allowing time and compounding to work on your behalf.

Today, we're going to start pulling those weeds.

The first step isn't changing your bank account.

The first step is changing your awareness.

As we continue clearing the soil, let's begin at the only place we can.

Where are you today?

Exercise

Take a moment to reflect on the healthy habits you've already cultivated.

Maybe you've committed to exercising, eating nourishing foods, reading personal development books, praying, meditating, journaling, or surrounding yourself with uplifting people. Pause for a moment and write them down. Celebrate how far you've already come.

Now, let's bring that same awareness to your finances.

Creating extraordinary wealth begins with knowing where you stand today. For many people, this is one of the hardest exercises in the entire book. Not because the math is difficult, but because fear convinces us not to look.

We avoid opening our bank accounts. We avoid checking balances. We avoid adding everything together because we believe what we don't see can't hurt us.

Today, we choose awareness over avoidance.

Today, we shine a light on every dollar, every asset, every debt, and every opportunity.

Awareness dissolves fear.

Once you know your numbers, they lose their power over you. What once felt overwhelming becomes measurable. What becomes measurable becomes manageable.

Then something beautiful happens.

We wrap every number in gratitude.

Gratitude shifts us from focusing on what's missing to recognizing what's already been entrusted to us. Wealth consciousness doesn't begin when you have more. It begins the moment you appreciate what you already have.

Before we can grow your financial garden, we must first understand the condition of the soil.

What Is Your Net Worth?

Your net worth is one of the most important numbers you'll ever know because it provides a clear snapshot of your financial health today.

Think of it as your financial scoreboard.

It isn't designed to shame you.

It's designed to guide you.

Your net worth is simply the total value of everything you own minus everything you owe.

Assets − Liabilities = Net Worth

Assets

Your assets are everything that adds value to your financial life, including:

- Checking and savings accounts
- Retirement accounts
- Investments
- Cryptocurrency
- Real estate
- Businesses
- Vehicles
- Cash
- Any other items of financial value

Liabilities

Your liabilities are everything you owe, including:

- Mortgage

- Vehicle loans
- Credit cards
- Student loans
- Personal loans
- Medical bills
- Taxes owed
- Any other outstanding debt

Example:

Assets

Savings Account: **$25,000**

Home Value: **$150,000**

Retirement Accounts: **$50,000**

Investments: **$10,000**

Total Assets = $235,000

Liabilities

Mortgage: **$120,000**

Vehicle Loan: **$15,000**

Credit Card Debt: **$5,000**

Total Liabilities = $140,000

Net Worth

$235,000 – $140,000 = $95,000

In this example, your net worth is **$95,000**.

Some of you will discover your net worth is positive.

Some of you will discover it's negative.

Both are perfectly okay.

This number is not your identity.

It is not your value.

It is simply your starting point.

Every thriving garden starts exactly where it is.

Bring loving awareness to your financial life today so you can celebrate every step forward tomorrow.

Remember:

What you measure, you improve.

One thing I've learned from studying successful entrepreneurs and investors is this:

High-level CEOs know their numbers.

They don't hope their business is profitable.

They know.

They review financial statements, cash flow, profit margins, and key performance indicators because numbers tell the truth.

Think about it this way.

Fans watch the scoreboard.

CEOs study the scorecard.

If you're serious about creating extraordinary wealth, you must know your numbers.

You are the CEO of your financial life.

Just as a gardener walks the land before planting the first seed, we're walking through your financial garden. Once you know where you're starting, you can confidently create a plan for where you're going.

I encourage you to calculate your net worth every month. (at least) I do this daily! Sometimes, multiple times a day. You will too!!

Begin to Watch it. Celebrate it. Track it. Learn from it.

Watching this number grow becomes one of the most rewarding parts of your wealth-building journey because every wise financial decision plants another seed for your future.

There will be seasons when your net worth rises.

There may also be seasons when markets fluctuate and it temporarily declines.

Don't panic. Learn to stay calm in the chaos, you are an investor now. The biggest upswings come after the darkness.

Stay rooted. Stay the course.

Volatility is part of investing, not proof that you're failing. We'll explore this more in later chapters.

Remember...

Your income tells you how much money you earn.

Your net worth tells you how much wealth you've built.

One measures what flows in.

The other measures what you've chosen to keep, grow, and faithfully steward.

What you measure, you improve.

What you nurture, grows.

Your Financial Garden Worksheet

Download the **Financial Garden Worksheet** from the Resources section and create your own personal net worth spreadsheet.

Organize your assets and liabilities to calculate your current net worth. I've included a completed example to guide you through the process.

Reflection Moment

Take a deep breath.

Remember, this number does not define your worth. It simply reveals the current condition of your financial garden.

There is no shame in your starting point.

There is only awareness. And awareness is where transformation begins.

Today, you pulled your first weeds by replacing avoidance with clarity.

From this moment forward, you'll never have to wonder where you stand. You'll know.

Every extraordinary garden begins with understanding the condition of the soil.

Every extraordinary investor begins by knowing their numbers.

The truth doesn't limit your future.

It illuminates the path toward it.

Congratulations!!!

You've just taken one of the most important steps toward becoming the CEO of your financial life.

CHAPTER 3

Laying the Foundation

"The best way to predict the future is to create it."

— Peter Drucker

The Vision. The Dream. The Mission.

Now that you've prepared the soil and pulled the weeds, it's time to decide what you're going to plant.

Every extraordinary life begins with a vision.

Every thriving business begins with a dream.

Every meaningful legacy begins with a mission.

The tragedy is that most people spend their entire lives building someone else's dream because they've never given themselves permission to define their own.

Read that sentence again.

Are you building someone else's dream?

If I handed you one hundred million dollars today, what would you do with it?

Yes...one hundred million dollars.

Not one million.

One hundred million.

You're reading a book written by Jenny Connolley.

We don't play small around here.

Close your eyes for just a moment and imagine someone deposited one hundred million dollars into your bank account today.

What would you do?

Of course you'd buy a beautiful home. You'd travel the world. You'd pay off every debt. You'd bless your family. You'd finally experience the freedom you've dreamed about for years.

There is absolutely nothing wrong with enjoying the blessings God has placed in your life.

Now keep going.

Don't stop there.

That's the easy answer.

I don't want the answer that comes from your current circumstances.

I want the answer that comes from your soul.

The answer you've been too afraid to say out loud.

The dream you've whispered about in private.

The dream that feels impossible.

The assignment you've talked yourself out of because it seemed too big, too expensive, too unrealistic, or too far away.

Today, we're breaking that ceiling.

No...

Today, we're shattering it.

I refuse to let you build another life based on limitations.

For the next few minutes, remove money from the equation.

Remove fear.

Remove doubt.

Remove every excuse you've ever told yourself about why you can't.

Now answer these questions.

Why did God place you on this earth?

What problem were you born to solve?

Who is waiting for your courage?

Who is praying for someone exactly like you and doesn't even know your name yet?

What assignment has God been preparing you for while you've been busy convincing yourself that it could never happen?

Don't tell me what seems realistic.

Tell me what burns inside of you.

Tell me what makes your heart race.

Tell me what you'd spend the rest of your life building, even if no one ever applauded you.

God did not create you simply to survive your life.

He didn't create you to pay bills, survive Mondays, retire someday, and quietly leave this world.

He created you to leave fingerprints on eternity.

He created you with gifts, passions, and experiences that no one else possesses in quite the same way. Every challenge you've faced, every heartbreak you've endured, every disappointment, every setback, every victory, every lesson—they've all been shaping you.

Even the things you wish had never happened.

The shitty parents.

The betrayal.

The loss.

The rejection.

The failures.

The moments that nearly broke you.

None of it was wasted.

Because your greatest wounds often become the doorway to someone else's healing.

The fire you survived becomes the fire you help someone else walk through.

The mountain you climbed becomes the map you hand to the next person.

That's how purpose works.

God doesn't waste pain.

He redeems it.

He multiplies it.

He uses it.

To heal.

To build.

To create.

To lead.

To serve.

To multiply what He has entrusted to you.

Your vision has always been bigger than you because it was never just about you.

It was always about the people whose lives will be different because you had the courage to answer the call.

Maybe this wasn't happening *to* you.

Maybe it was happening *through* you.

For them.

For such a time as this.

And here's the wild part...

On some level, your soul already knew.

You signed up for this.

So do it!! Dream so freakin big that the only explanation for your success is God.

There is a beautiful Japanese philosophy called **Ikigai**, often translated as "your reason for being." I love that idea because I believe every one of us was created with a divine assignment.

God placed unique gifts inside of you, gave you experiences no one else has lived, and planted a calling that only you can fulfill. Somewhere between what you love, what you're gifted at, what the world desperately needs, and how you can serve others is the work you were created to do.

That is your Golden Garden.

For me, wealth has never been about collecting more things.

Wealth is about becoming a faithful steward of the resources God entrusts to me so I can answer the calling He has placed on my life.

I see foundations around the world where horses once destined for slaughter run free for the rest of their lives.

I see children rescued from sex trafficking finding safety, healing, and hope because someone refused to look away.

I see young adults aging out of foster care walking across graduation stages, starting businesses, buying homes, and discovering that their past never determined their future.

I see women rising from depression, anxiety, addiction, and suicidal thoughts to become leaders, mothers, entrepreneurs, and lights in their communities because someone reminded them who they truly are.

That is why I am building wealth.

Not for a bigger bank account.

Not for more things.

Not for status.

Every dollar becomes another opportunity to serve, another horse rescued, another child protected, another family restored, another dream funded, another life forever changed.

Money has never been my mission.

Money is the resource that allows my mission to expand.

Now it's your turn.

If every financial limitation disappeared tomorrow, what would you build?

Who would you become?

Whose life would be different because you had the courage to say yes?

See it so clearly that you can feel it.

Speak it with absolute conviction.

Write it down.

Pray over it.

Read it every single day until your vision becomes stronger than your fear.

It's time to break through your wealth thermostat.

It's time to hold a higher vision.

Because somewhere inside of you is a Golden Garden that only you were created to plant.

And this...

Now do this.

Seriously... put the book down.

Don't wait until tomorrow. Don't tell yourself you'll come back to it later. Do it right now.

I don't want you writing your vision yet.

I want you to speak it.

Open the voice recorder on your phone and start talking. I find writing is too slow for my brain. When I speak, conviction, passion, and truth come pouring out with every breath. My heart always knows where it's going long before my pen can catch up.

Don't edit yourself.

Don't overthink it.

Don't worry if it sounds messy.

Just let it flow.

Speak the vision God has placed on your heart. Speak the dream you've been afraid to say out loud. Speak the mission you know you were created to fulfill.

Then listen to it.

Listen again.

And again.

Until your vision becomes louder than your fear.

If you're feeling really bold, send me a DM on Facebook or Instagram. I'd love to hear your heart, celebrate your vision, and cheer you on as you begin building your Golden Garden.

This moment matters more than you realize. Love you.

CHAPTER 4

Tools before the Planting

"Give me six hours to chop down a tree and I will spend the first four sharpening the axe."

— Abraham Lincoln

Before We Plant: Gather Your Garden Tools

Every experienced gardener knows that before planting a single seed, you gather the right tools. The same is true when you're building wealth.

Over the last few chapters, you've prepared the soil by healing old wounds, pulling the weeds of scarcity, and creating a vision for the life you're called to live. Now it's time to prepare yourself, because the greatest investment you'll ever make isn't in the stock market.

It's in the person making the decisions.

You.

Before we begin planting the seeds that will grow into your financial future, I want to place four powerful tools in your hands. These are practices that have shaped my own life, strengthened my mindset, and helped me become the woman capable of receiving and stewarding greater abundance.

These aren't just investing tools.

They'rc life tools.

They'll help you stay grounded when fear shows up, remind you of who you are when doubt creeps in, and keep your heart focused on what truly matters.

As you continue tending your financial garden, I encourage you to return to these practices often.

They've become part of my daily life, and I believe they'll become part of yours too.

In this section, we'll explore:

- **Your Soul Mission and Purpose**: Never lose sight of why you're building wealth in the first place.
- **The Gratitude Practice**: Train your mind to recognize abundance instead of scarcity.
- **The Confidence Résumé**: Create a written reminder of the strength, resilience, and wisdom you've already earned.

- **The Confidence Anchor**: A simple technique to help you return to peace, confidence, and clarity whenever emotions threaten to take over.

Let's gather our tools before we plant.

Tool #1: Your Soul Mission

Never forget this:

Money is the tool.

Your mission is the reason.

When your "why" is clear, your financial decisions become easier. Every investment becomes intentional because it's connected to something far greater than simply making more money.

Build wealth with purpose, and your harvest will always be richer than your bank account.

Recording this and Listen in your Voice= Pure Magic!

Tool #2: Practice Radical Gratitude

One of the most valuable practices I learned early in my wealth journey came from the incredible Linda P. Jones.

It's simple.

It's completely free.

And it has the power to change the way you see your entire life.

Most people believe they'll feel abundant once they have more money.

I've discovered the opposite is true.

Abundance begins the moment you recognize how much you've already been given.

I want you to write down one hundred things you're grateful for.

Yes...one hundred. **100**

You'll probably fly through the first twenty or thirty. Then your brain will start telling you that you've run out of things to write.

Keep Going, don’t stop, let the pen flow.

That's when the exercise begins doing its greatest work.

Look around.

Notice what you've been overlooking.

Your heartbeat.

Clean water.

The roof over your head.

Food in your refrigerator.

The sunrise.

Your children.

Your pets.

A friend who always answers the phone.

Your favorite coffee mug.

The smell of fresh rain.

Keep writing until you reach one hundred.

Somewhere around number forty or fifty, something beautiful begins to happen. You stop searching for the big things and start appreciating the small blessings that have quietly surrounded you all along.

By the time you reach one hundred, you'll realize you've been living in abundance this entire time.

Gratitude shifts your focus from what you lack to everything you've already been given.

That's where true wealth begins.

Your Gratitude Practice

1. Find a quiet place where you won't be interrupted.
2. Take three slow, deep breaths and allow your body to relax.
3. Write down one hundred things you're grateful for.
4. Read your list out loud, allowing yourself to feel each blessing.
5. Close your eyes for a few moments and simply receive the richness that's already present in your life.

6. Return to this practice anytime fear, scarcity, comparison, or worry begin taking root.

Remember, what you focus on expands.

Tool #3: Create Your Confidence Résumé

One of the greatest gifts I've ever received came from my dear friend, Molly Smith.

She introduced me to a practice she calls the **Confidence Résumé**, and I can honestly say it changed the way I see myself.

Molly shared it with me as I began my sobriety journey which i was unsuccessful at unit May 5, 2025. Something clicked! I finally released it. I just celebrated one full year alcohol-free!!. It was the result of healing, choosing myself every day, and doing the inner work that lasting transformation requires. Took me many, many, many restarts. Yet I kept swinging and now alcohol is simply a past of my past.

My Confidence Résumé became one of the tools that carried me through those seasons.

Whenever self-doubt whispers that I'm not enough...

I read it.

Whenever I forget how far I've come...

I read it.

Whenever life feels heavy...

I read it.

Because confidence isn't something you find.

It's something you remember.

Your Confidence Résumé is exactly what it sounds like: a written reminder of the incredible person you've already become.

Write down every victory you've achieved.

Every hardship you've overcome.

Every challenge you've survived.

Every lesson you've learned.

Every life you've impacted.

Every skill you've developed.

Every God-given gift you've been blessed with.

Celebrate yourself.

Build yourself up until it feels just a little uncomfortable.

Then print it.

Frame it.

Read it often.

Whenever I read mine, one thought always comes to mind.

Come try me.

Not because I think life will be easy.

Because I know what I've already survived. Seriously! Come try me, what you got!!

My Confidence Résumé reminds me that there is nothing life can place in front of me that God and I can't walk through together.

The same is true for you.

Every challenge you've overcome has strengthened your character.

Every obstacle has built your resilience.

Every scar tells a story of courage.

Those battle wounds aren't something to hide.

They're your credentials.

Never forget how far you've already come.

How to Create Your Confidence Résumé

1. Light a candle and create a peaceful environment.
2. Set aside one uninterrupted hour with a journal and pen.
3. List everything you've created, including your family, home, businesses, and accomplishments.
4. List every hardship you've overcome and every season you've survived.
5. Write down your gifts, strengths, talents, and skills.
6. Reflect on the person you've become because of everything you've experienced.

7. If you'd like, use ChatGPT or Claude to transform your list into powerful "I Am" affirmations.

8. Print it, frame it, and read it every morning.

Tool #4: Create Your Confidence Anchor

Finally, I want to leave you with one simple technique I use whenever emotions begin influencing my decisions.

Think of a time when you felt calm, confident, and completely certain about your future. Picture the version of yourself who makes wise financial decisions with patience, discipline, and peace.

As you hold that feeling, gently press your thumb and middle finger together while taking a slow, deep breath. Allow that confidence to settle into your body.

Practice this several times, and your brain will begin associating that simple gesture with a calm, confident emotional state.

Then, whenever fear creeps in, the market becomes volatile, or doubt begins whispering in your ear, simply press those two fingers together again.

Pause.

Breathe.

Reconnect with the person you're becoming.

The goal isn't to ignore what's happening around you.

The goal is to respond with wisdom instead of emotion.

Great investors make decisions from clarity, not fear.

Never forget that your greatest investment will always be the person making the decisions.

CHAPTER 5

Seek the Mentor

"It's good to learn from your mistakes. It's better to learn from other people's mistakes."

— Warren Buffett

Find Someone Who Can Shorten Your Journey

One of the greatest lessons I've learned in business, investing, and life is this:

Success leaves clues.

Whatever you're hoping to achieve, someone else has already walked that path. They've made the mistakes, learned the lessons, weathered the storms, and discovered what works.

Why spend years trying to figure it all out on your own when someone else has already left a trail?

My journey into this new financial garden began in 2017 when a friend and soon-to-be business partner introduced me to Bitcoin. At the time, it was trading for around $3,000 a coin.

What a ride.

The market never closed. It traded 24 hours a day, seven days a week, and I found myself checking prices at all hours. As Bitcoin climbed toward $20,000, I became completely fascinated. If I'm being honest, I was a little obsessed.

I had purchased my first Bitcoin around $3,500, and watching the market move in real time was both exhilarating and humbling. Some days it felt like the future had arrived. Other days it felt like complete chaos. Holy moly, what a rollercoaster!

Having spent two years as a Casino Host, I wasn't interested in gambling. I'd seen how that story usually ends. I wanted to understand what I owned. I wanted to know why this technology had captured the attention of investors around the world and why it could move so dramatically.

Thankfully, I wasn't trying to figure it out alone.

During our move from California to Texas, I became a devoted listener of Linda P. Jones' *Be Wealthy & Smart* podcast. I loved the way she taught investing. She had a gift for making complex financial concepts feel approachable, practical, and empowering.

One day she briefly mentioned a digital asset she had been researching. She only touched on it for a few minutes, yet something inside me leaned in. My curiosity was sparked.

Around that same time, Linda had released her first book, and I was fortunate enough to win both a copy and a thirty-minute coaching call with her. Looking back, I know that moment was spirit-led.

I still remember how excited and nervous I felt before that call.

I came prepared with pages of questions. My husband, Tom, quietly sat in the background listening to every word.

By the end of our conversation, I knew I had found the mentor I had been searching for.

There was no pressure. No sales pitch. Just wisdom, integrity, and years of experience I knew I could learn from.

When I shared the details of her membership with Tom, he looked at me and said something I'll never forget.

"Do it, Babe."

That simple sentence changed the trajectory of our financial future.

Joining Linda's community became one of the greatest investments I have ever made in myself, behind Marrying Tom of course!

Her education transformed the way I thought about investing. Instead of reacting to headlines or listening to the loudest voices on television, I learned how to research projects for myself. I learned to ask better questions. I learned to invest with conviction instead of emotion. I learned how to remain calm under extreme volatility while seeing through illusions and distractions.

More importantly, I discovered **The greatest investment you'll ever make isn't in a stock, a business, real estate, or even cryptocurrency.**

It's in your own education.

Knowledge creates confidence.

Confidence leads to better decisions.

Better decisions create better outcomes.

That's the real return on investment.

I will always be grateful for the role Linda P. Jones played in my investing journey. Her wisdom, integrity, and passion for financial education gave me the confidence to think independently and invest with conviction.

If you'd like to continue expanding your financial knowledge after reading this book, I've included Linda's resources, along with many of my other favorite books, podcasts, and educational tools, in the Resources section at the back of this book.

Because one mentor, one conversation, or one book has the power to change the direction of your life.

Mine certainly did.

How to Find a Great Mentor

- Look for someone who teaches with integrity, not hype.
- Choose someone who educates rather than predicts.
- Invest in learning before investing more money.
- Stay teachable. Curiosity is one of your greatest assets.
- Remember that mentors don't always meet you in person. Sometimes they're found through books, podcasts, courses, or communities.

Chapter Reflection

Preparing the soil isn't about changing who you are.

It's about uncovering who you've been all along.

Every experience you've lived through, every belief you've inherited, every challenge you've faced, and every lesson you've learned has shaped the person standing here today. Some of those experiences have strengthened your roots. Others have planted weeds that no longer belong in your garden.

Now you have a choice.

You can continue living from the stories that were handed to you, or you can begin writing a new story rooted in purpose, faith, and possibility.

That's where true wealth begins.

Not in a stock portfolio.

Not in a bank account.

Not in the size of your paycheck.

It begins with the person making the decisions.

As you'll discover throughout this book, money is simply a tool. In the hands of someone living with fear, it magnifies fear. In the hands of someone living with purpose, it becomes a powerful force for good.

My prayer is that you won't simply learn how to build wealth.

I hope you'll become the kind of person God can trust with it.

Because we're living through one of the greatest opportunities in history. More women than ever before are stepping into positions of financial leadership, creating businesses, building investments, and leaving legacies for generations to come.

That excites me, not because of the money, but because of what's possible.

I see women changing family trees.

I see children growing up with financial wisdom instead of financial fear.

I see communities strengthened by generous hearts.

I see lives transformed because one woman decided to believe she was created for more.

That's why preparing the soil matters.

The harvest you'll experience tomorrow is determined by the seeds you choose to plant today.

So let's keep tending the garden.

The best is still to come.

PART II

PLANT

PART II: PLANT

Wisdom from Solomon

"Sow your seed in the morning, and at evening let your hands not be idle, for you do not know which will succeed, whether this or that, or whether both will do equally well."
— Ecclesiastes 11:6

King Solomon understood a principle that has guided farmers for thousands of years. A farmer never knows exactly which seed will produce the greatest harvest. One field may flourish while another struggles, and one season may produce an abundant crop while another requires patience. Even so, the wise farmer continues planting because he knows that a harvest is only possible if the seeds are first placed into the ground.

The same principle applies to building wealth.

Every investment you make is a seed planted for your future. Some investments will exceed your expectations, while others may take years to reveal their true potential. No one can predict the future with certainty, but every successful investor understands that consistent planting creates the opportunity for future abundance.

In this section of the book, you'll learn the principles of becoming a wise investor. We'll explore how to recognize opportunity, develop conviction through education, build a strategy you can follow with confidence, and understand why consistency often produces greater results than trying to perfectly time the market.

Most importantly, I hope you'll begin thinking like a farmer instead of a speculator. Farmers don't wake up every morning expecting a harvest. They wake up ready to tend the fields, trusting that today's faithful work will produce tomorrow's reward.

My hope is that by the end of this section, you'll have both the knowledge and the confidence to begin planting your own financial garden, one seed at a time, while allowing time and consistency to do what they have always done best.

Let's begin planting.

CHAPTER 6

Our New Financial Garden

"Luck is what happens when preparation meets opportunity."

— Seneca

Before I share the seeds I've planted in my own financial garden, I want you to understand why I chose them.

My goal isn't to convince you to invest in anything simply because I did. My goal is to teach you how to think, not what to think.

Stay curious. Ask questions. Challenge assumptions. Do your own research.

If this chapter inspires you to become a lifelong student of the financial world, then I've accomplished exactly what I set out to do.

Everything I'm about to share comes from my own investing journey, thousands of hours of research, years of studying the financial markets, and the wisdom I've gained from incredible mentors along the way.

I don't pretend to have all the answers, and I never will. The financial world is constantly evolving, which means there is always more to learn. That's one of the reasons I love investing. Every day offers a new lesson, a new perspective, or another piece of the puzzle waiting to be discovered.

One of the greatest blessings of the world we live in today is that we have access to an incredible amount of financial education. There are brilliant investors, economists, and educators who dive much deeper into many of the topics we'll touch on in this chapter.

This chapter isn't meant to teach you everything there is to know about investing. It's designed to give you a foundation, a new perspective, and the confidence to continue learning long after you've finished this book.

Early in my investing journey, I realized I had been asking the wrong question. Instead of asking, *"What's the hottest investment?"* or *"What coin is everyone buying?"* I started asking, **"What problem is this trying to solve?"**

That one question led me down a rabbit hole of research that completely changed the way I viewed money, technology, and the future of finance. I realized that every meaningful investment begins with understanding the problem it's designed to solve.

Why Does All of This Matter?

Have you ever stopped to think about how money actually moves around the world?

Most of us never do. We tap a credit card, send money through Venmo or Zelle, pay a bill online, or wire funds across the country, and we expect it to work. We rarely think about everything happening behind the scenes or how many financial institutions are involved before that money reaches its destination.

The truth is, the global financial system that moves trillions of dollars every year was built decades ago. While it has served us well, it was designed long before smartphones, online banking, digital wallets, and instant payments became part of everyday life.

Imagine trying to stream your favorite Netflix series using dial-up internet. It would eventually work, but it certainly wouldn't be the fastest or most efficient way to do it.

That's a good way to think about much of today's financial infrastructure. It still works, but it's slow, expensive, and outdated.

Every year, more than $190 trillion moves between banks, businesses, governments, and financial institutions around the world. Many of those transactions pass through multiple intermediaries before reaching their final destination, adding time, cost, and unnecessary complexity along the way.

As technology has evolved, it has become clear that our financial system needs to evolve too.

Thankfully, it is.

One of the biggest changes happening today is the global adoption of **ISO 20022**.

I know... it sounds like the name of a robot or some secret government project.

I promise it's much simpler than that.

Let's start with the basics.

What the Heck Is ISO 20022?

ISO 20022 is a new global messaging standard that helps banks, payment providers, and financial institutions communicate with one another more clearly and efficiently.

Notice I said **messaging standard**.

It isn't a cryptocurrency.

It isn't a digital currency.

It isn't a new banking system.

Think of it as a new language that financial institutions around the world are learning to speak.

Imagine trying to have a conversation with someone who speaks a completely different language. Communication is slower, misunderstandings happen, and important details can easily get lost.

Now imagine everyone speaking the same language.

Everything becomes faster, clearer, and more efficient.

That's exactly what ISO 20022 is doing for the financial world.

For decades, banks have been sending payment information using an older messaging format that was created long before smartphones, online banking, and today's digital economy. It served its purpose, but it wasn't designed for the digital world we live in today.

ISO 20022 changes that by allowing financial institutions to send richer, more detailed payment information. That means fewer processing errors, stronger fraud detection, more efficient compliance, better data analysis, and faster payments.

Here's the key takeaway:

ISO 20022 isn't changing our money. It's changing how financial institutions communicate about money.

The U.S. dollar, the euro, the British pound, the Japanese yen, and many other fiat currencies can all use the ISO 20022 standard. It's simply a smarter, more efficient way for banks and financial institutions to exchange information.

You may never hear your bank talk about ISO 20022, but there's a good chance you'll benefit from it. As more financial institutions adopt the standard, payments can become faster, more secure, more accurate, and easier to process around the world.

Think of it like upgrading from sending a fax to sending an email. The information hasn't changed. The way it's sent has. It's faster, clearer, and much more efficient.

While traditional banks were upgrading the way they communicate, another revolutionary technology was quietly emerging alongside it.

The two are often mentioned together, but they serve very different purposes.

ISO 20022 improves communication.

Blockchain transforms the way information is securely recorded, verified, and shared.

Together, they're helping shape the future of finance.

That brings us to our next question.

What the Heck Is Blockchain?

If cryptocurrency is digital money, then blockchain is the technology that makes it all possible.

I like to think of blockchain as Google Docs for financial records.

Imagine thousands of people all looking at the same document at the same time. Everyone can see the latest updates, everyone is working from the same version, and no single person secretly controls the master copy.

Blockchain works in a similar way.

Instead of relying on one bank, one company, or one government to keep the records, thousands of computers around the world each maintain an identical copy of the same digital ledger.

Think of that ledger as a giant digital record book that keeps track of every transaction ever made.

Every time a new transaction takes place, the network works together to verify it's accurate before adding it to the ledger. Once it's recorded, changing it becomes incredibly difficult because every copy of the ledger would have to be changed at the same time.

That's one of the reasons blockchain is considered so secure.

The internet changed how we share information.

Blockchain is changing how we store, verify, and transfer value.

When I finally understood blockchain, I realized cryptocurrency wasn't just another investment. It was part of a much bigger technological shift with the potential to transform finance, business, healthcare, supply chains, real estate, digital identity, and countless other industries.

That was a turning point for me.

I stopped seeing blockchain as a passing trend and started seeing it as one of the most important technological innovations of our generation.

Naturally, my next question became:

If blockchain is the technology, then what exactly is cryptocurrency?

What the Heck Is Cryptocurrency?

Let's make this simple because people tend to overcomplicate it.

Cryptocurrency is digital money that exists on the internet. Instead of being managed by a single bank or government, it operates on blockchain technology, where thousands of computers around the world work together to verify and record every transaction.

Think of cryptocurrency as money that got an internet upgrade.

Just as email transformed the way we send letters, cryptocurrency is transforming the way value moves around the world. It allows people to send and receive money directly, often faster, with greater transparency, and without relying on a single institution to process every transaction.

Another way to think about it is this: the internet changed how we share information, and cryptocurrency is changing how we exchange value.

One of the biggest misconceptions is that every cryptocurrency is trying to replace traditional money. While a handful were created with that goal in mind, many others were built to serve completely different purposes. Some help move money across borders more efficiently, others power decentralized applications and smart contracts, while others are designed to improve digital identity, supply chains, gaming, or countless other industries.

That's why there are thousands of different cryptocurrencies. They aren't all competing to do the same job. They're attempting to solve different problems, support different technologies, and create new possibilities in an increasingly digital world.

Like any emerging technology, some projects will succeed, some will fail, and many will disappear altogether. That's a normal part of innovation. We saw the same thing happen during the early days of the internet. Hundreds of companies came and went before the strongest ideas emerged and transformed the way we live.

Understanding that helped me see cryptocurrency differently. It wasn't just about digital coins. It was about a new wave of technology that is still evolving and helping shape the future of finance and beyond.

Now, let's take a look at some of the seeds I chose to plant in my own Golden Garden.

CHAPTER 7

Choosing the Seeds

"Someone is sitting in the shade today because someone planted a tree a long time ago."

— Warren Buffett

Okay, friends...

This is the chapter I've been most excited to share.

Everything we've explored so far has prepared your Golden Garden. We've cleared the weeds of fear, enriched the soil with knowledge, and created a strong foundation for long-term growth.

Now comes one of the most exciting parts of the journey.

It's time to choose the seeds.

Before we begin, I encourage you to become a student of the projects that capture your attention. Read beyond the headlines. Explore the technology, the leadership-CEO's, the partnerships, the adoption, and the real-world problems each project is working to solve.

The more you understand *why* a project exists, the more confidence you'll have in the decisions you make.

One important point deserves clarification.

ISO 20022 is a global financial messaging standard. It creates a common language that allows financial institutions to exchange information more efficiently. It is not a cryptocurrency, and there is no official list of "ISO-approved" digital assets.

Several blockchain companies, however, are building technology designed to integrate with this evolving financial infrastructure.

That distinction changed the way I approached my research.

Instead of searching for an "ISO coin," I began asking deeper questions.

What problem does this project solve?

Who is using the technology?

Is adoption expanding?

Does the leadership have a clear long-term vision?

How could this technology contribute to the future of finance?

Those questions became my compass.

As my research deepened and my conversations with mentors continued, five projects consistently rose to the surface. Each focuses on a different area of the financial ecosystem—global payments, financial inclusion, enterprise infrastructure, tokenized assets, or international trade.

Together, they represent five different seeds with five different purposes.

Out of the thousands of digital assets that exist today, these are the TOP 5 that earned a place in my Golden Garden.

🌱 XRP

The Bridge for Global Money

Every day, trillions of dollars move across international borders.

Many of those transactions still travel through systems built decades ago, passing through multiple financial institutions before reaching their destination. The process often requires significant liquidity, multiple intermediaries, and valuable time.

XRP introduces a faster path.

Designed as a bridge between currencies, XRP allows value to move across the world in seconds while improving efficiency for cross-border settlement.

Ripple, the company closely associated with XRP, has spent years building payment infrastructure for financial institutions while developing solutions that align with the ISO 20022 financial messaging standard.

The more I explored Ripple's technology, partnerships, and long-term vision, the more I appreciated the scale of the opportunity.

Global payments represent one of the largest financial markets in the world. Technology that improves speed, efficiency, and liquidity naturally captured my attention.

If you only look here, You'll be a Winner (Just my Opinion, NOT FACTS)

🌱 Stellar Lumens (XLM)

Expanding Financial Access

Financial opportunity has the power to transform lives.

The Stellar network focuses on making payments fast, affordable, and accessible for people around the world. Its technology connects digital assets with traditional currencies while helping individuals and businesses access financial services through local institutions.

What inspired me most was Stellar's mission.

Millions of people continue building businesses, supporting families, and pursuing opportunities with limited access to modern financial services. Stellar is creating infrastructure that opens more doors, expands economic participation, and helps connect more people to the global economy.

🌱 Hedera (HBAR)

Building Enterprise Infrastructure

As blockchain technology continues to evolve, enterprise adoption has the potential to shape its next chapter.

Hedera was created with that future in mind.

Its distributed ledger technology delivers speed, security, scalability, and energy efficiency while supporting applications across payments, digital identity, artificial intelligence, healthcare, supply-chain management, and tokenized assets.

One aspect immediately stood out to me—its governance.

A council of globally recognized organizations provides oversight and long-term stewardship, creating a foundation built on stability, accountability, and trust.

Reliable infrastructure forms the backbone of every modern economy, and Hedera is developing technology designed to support that future.

🌱 Ondo Finance (ONDO)

Bridging Traditional Finance and Blockchain

Some of the greatest innovations build bridges between existing systems and emerging technology.

Ondo Finance focuses on bringing real-world assets onto blockchain networks through tokenization. Financial products connected to U.S. Treasury securities and other traditional assets become easier to own, transfer, divide, and access digitally.

The idea immediately fascinated me, especially when I noticed the process is already beginning.

Blockchain technology has the potential to complement traditional finance by creating greater efficiency, transparency, and accessibility while preserving many of the financial tools people already know and trust.

That vision continues to make Ondo one of the most interesting projects I've studied. This could be a #2, I really love it!

🌱 XDC Network (XDC)

Modernizing Global Trade

Global trade connects nations, businesses, and communities every single day.

Behind every shipment lies a complex network of paperwork, approvals, payments, and financial agreements. Many of those systems continue to rely on processes developed decades ago.

The XDC Network focuses on bringing greater speed and efficiency to trade finance through blockchain technology.

Its infrastructure supports business payments, tokenized assets, trade documentation, and digital settlement while improving transparency throughout the process.

As global commerce becomes increasingly digital, infrastructure that simplifies international trade has the potential to become an important part of tomorrow's financial system.

These five projects each address a different challenge.

Together, they reminded me that the future of finance will likely grow through collaboration, innovation, and many technologies working side by side.

That's exactly how a healthy garden grows.

One seed alone creates a plant.

Many carefully chosen seeds create an ecosystem.

Choosing Seeds with Intention

One of the greatest lessons I've learned as a savvy investor is that not every digital asset is trying to accomplish the same thing.

That's easy to forget when you first get into this space because everything gets lumped together under the word *crypto*. But once you start digging a little deeper, you realize each project has its own purpose.

Some are trying to make global payments faster and cheaper.

Some are connecting traditional finance with blockchain technology.

Some are bringing real-world assets onto the blockchain.

Others are working to modernize international trade.

Each one is planting a different seed.

That's why I've never been interested in buying something just because someone on social media says it's "going to the moon." That isn't investing. That's chasing hype.

I want to know what the project actually does.

I want to know what problem it's solving.

I want to know who's using it and whether adoption is growing.

I want to know if the leadership has a vision that's still going to matter ten years from now.

Those are the kinds of questions that helped me build my own Golden Garden, and I encourage you to ask those same questions every time you're considering a new investment.

Now, does that mean every seed you plant is going to grow?

Of course not.

If only investing were that easy.

Some seeds grow into massive trees.

Some take years before they break through the soil.

And some never grow at all.

That's investing.

None of us has a crystal ball, and anyone who tells you they know exactly what's going to happen is selling certainty that simply doesn't exist.

What I do know is this. I believe we're still early.

Blockchain technology is continuing to evolve, and every year we see more banks, businesses, governments, and financial institutions exploring how to use it in the real world. If that trend continues, I believe the projects solving real problems today could become part of tomorrow's financial infrastructure.

As I sit here writing this book, these are approximately what the five digital assets in my Golden Garden are worth:

- XRP – $1.07
- XLM – $0.17
- HBAR – $0.0704
- ONDO – $0.372
- XDC – $0.0260

Will those prices be higher by the time you read this years from now?

I certainly hope so.

None of us knows what the future holds, but that's part of what makes investing so exciting.

Maybe one day we'll both look back at this page and smile.

Maybe we'll laugh and say, "Can you believe we were looking at these projects when they were still seeds?"

That thought genuinely excites me.

We're documenting a moment in time before the story has been written.

Whether these five projects become some of the biggest winners or whether another project eventually earns a place in your Golden Garden, my hope is that you walk away from this book thinking differently.

I don't want you to simply copy what I own.

I want you to become a savvy investor who knows how to evaluate opportunities for yourself.

Because that's a skill that can serve you for the rest of your life.

And just like any beautiful garden, extraordinary wealth doesn't appear overnight.

It grows one carefully chosen seed at a time.

My Core Seed

Spoiler Alert:

#1 Seed (by a Massive Landslide)=XRP

Understanding Ripple & XRP Through Companies You Already Know

If you know anything about me before reading this book, you already know which seed I have the strongest conviction in.

One of the biggest barriers I see for new investors is the feeling that they need to understand every technical detail before they can begin. The truth is, you probably use dozens of technologies every single day without understanding how they work behind the scenes.

You don't need to know how the internet routes data to send an email.

You don't need to understand cellular networks to make a phone call.

You don't need to know how cloud computing works to stream a movie on Netflix.

You simply use the technology because it works.

Investing often works the same way.

Throughout this chapter, I'm going to compare Ripple and XRP to companies you already know and trust. My goal isn't to make you a blockchain engineer. My goal is to help you understand the concepts well enough to see why I have such strong conviction.

This is where your mindset begins to shift from consumer to investor.

Consumers simply use products.

Investors ask, "Who built the technology that powers those products?"

That single question has created enormous wealth throughout history.

First, remember this distinction.

Ripple is the technology company.

XRP is the digital asset that operates within Ripple's ecosystem and can be used for liquidity and value transfer.

They are connected, yet they are different.

Think of them like these familiar companies.

Apple

Apple is the company.

The iPhone is one of its products.

Millions of people use an iPhone every day without owning a single share of Apple stock.

Likewise, millions of people could someday use payment systems that leverage XRP without ever realizing it.

The technology simply works behind the scenes.

Amazon

Amazon is the company.

Amazon Web Services (AWS) is one of its products.

Most people have never heard of AWS, yet it powers websites, hospitals, banks, governments, streaming services, airlines, and thousands of businesses around the world.

Most people never think about it because the infrastructure stays invisible.

Ripple's vision is similar.

One day, people may send money across the world in seconds without ever knowing XRP helped make it possible.

The only thing they'll notice is that their money arrived almost instantly.

Visa

Visa is the company.

Visa operates one of the largest payment networks in the world.

When you swipe your Visa card, Visa usually isn't sending your money. It is securely transmitting payment information between the merchant and financial institutions so the transaction can be authorized.

The actual movement and settlement of funds happens through banking infrastructure.

Ripple is focused on improving that settlement layer.

Instead of financial institutions waiting hours or even days to move value internationally, XRP can be used as a bridge asset to provide liquidity and help settle transactions in seconds.

FedEx

FedEx is the logistics company.

The package is what gets delivered.

Nobody says, "I'm investing in cardboard boxes."

The value is in the company that built the delivery network.

Ripple is building a network for moving value.

XRP is one of the assets that can travel through that network to help move money efficiently around the world.

Uber

Uber is the platform.

The cars belong to the drivers.

The platform connects everyone together.

Ripple is creating technology that connects financial institutions more efficiently.

XRP can serve as the bridge asset that helps value move between different currencies.

Netflix

Netflix is the company.

Movies are the content.

People subscribe because Netflix built a better way to deliver entertainment.

Ripple is building a better way for financial institutions to move money internationally.

XRP is one of the tools that can make that movement faster, cheaper, and more efficient.

Google

Google is the company.

Google Search is one product.

Google Maps is another.

Gmail is another.

Android is another.

A single company can create many products that solve different problems.

Ripple has developed multiple enterprise payment solutions over the years.

XRP is one component within the broader ecosystem, designed for specific use cases involving liquidity and cross-border value transfer.

Railroads

Imagine the 1800s.

Millions of people rode trains.

Very few people understood how railroads were financed.

The greatest fortunes weren't created by riding the train.

They were created by investing in the companies building the tracks.

Technology has always followed this pattern.

Most people become consumers first.

A much smaller group recognizes the infrastructure being built underneath.

Those are often the people who participate in the greatest wealth creation.

That is exactly how I look at Ripple and XRP. Infrastructure

This is a cryptocurrency dominant powerhouse!!

Ripple has developed payment technology and a digital asset (XRP) designed to help move value across borders with remarkable speed, efficiency and low cost.

XRP is fast, green and costs a fraction of a penny to send money.

Yes, every investment carries risk. The markets are highly manipulated and violated. That is why you layer yourself in knowledge to become unshakable.

What I can tell you with complete confidence is this: learning to identify the infrastructure being built beneath the world's financial system completely changed the my emotions around investing

Shifting from consumer to investor may become one of the most valuable mindset changes you ever make.

The Lawsuit and the Progression

When I started investing in XRP, the lawsuit was already underway.

XRP had been removed from several major U.S. exchanges, including Coinbase, and the only place I could purchase it was through Uphold. Everywhere I looked, people were talking about fear, uncertainty, doubt and the possibility that XRP would disappear.

At the time, there were hardly any positive videos on YouTube. Today, you can spend five minutes researching XRP and find countless interviews, news stories, and discussions about its future.

That alone shows how much has changed.

Thankfully, this was also the exact season I found Linda P. Jones and joined her private membership community. Instead of surrounding myself with people reacting to headlines and hype, I surrounded myself with people who were doing the research. We studied the technology, followed the court case, learned how our financial system actually works, and asked better questions.

There was something about XRP that kept pulling me in.

I can't fully explain it.

The more I learned, the more I felt I was exactly where I was supposed to be. Looking back now, I truly feel God was guiding me to this asset for a reason. It became much more than an investment. It became part of a mission I know I was called to fulfill during this lifetime.

It's also during this season that I accumulated the majority of my XRP holdings. While many investors were selling because fear had taken over the market, I was buying because my understanding kept growing.

Warren Buffett famously said, ***"Be fearful when others are greedy, and be greedy when others are fearful."*** That philosophy has stayed with me throughout my investing journey.

So what was the lawsuit actually about?

The SEC argued that certain sales of XRP should have followed the same securities laws that apply when a company sells shares of stock. Ripple argued that XRP is a digital asset with its own utility and should not automatically be treated the same as company stock.

After several years in court, the judge made an important distinction. The ruling explained that XRP itself is not inherently a security and that different types of XRP sales can be evaluated differently depending on how they are conducted. That distinction separated Ripple, the company, from XRP, the digital asset, and provided far more regulatory clarity than the industry had before.

As that clarity emerged, major U.S. exchanges, including Coinbase, relisted XRP. Regulators also began providing clearer guidance for digital assets, and **XRP is now widely recognized as one of the digital assets with the strongest regulatory clarity in the United States.**

At the same time, the financial industry continued moving toward blockchain technology. Organizations like the DTCC, which helps process and settle trillions of dollars in securities transactions, have been exploring tokenization and distributed ledger technology as a faster and more efficient way to move assets. Lawmakers have also been working to establish clearer rules through legislation like the GENIUS

Act and the proposed CLARITY Act. Together, these efforts are creating a stronger foundation for institutional adoption.

It's coming, friends!

Banks, governments, and large financial institutions move carefully. They build when there are clear rules. As regulatory uncertainty continues to fade, more institutions can confidently explore blockchain technology and digital assets.

For me, the lawsuit was never simply a headline. It was an invitation to learn. Every hour I spent researching strengthened my understanding of where the financial system is headed, and that's why XRP became one of the core seeds in my Golden Garden.

In Closing out this part of PLANT:

Take everything you've learned in this chapter and make it your invitation to go deeper.

Don't take my word for it.

Research it.

Question it.

Challenge it.

Learn from people who disagree with me.

Learn from people who agree with me. Read books. Watch interviews. Listen to podcasts. Study the technology. Follow the legislation. Pay attention to what governments, financial institutions, and the world's largest companies are doing.

Then come to your own conclusion.

I can't tell you what to invest in, and I wouldn't want to. My intention is to educate, inspire curiosity, and encourage you to become an informed investor who makes decisions from knowledge instead of fear.

I'm just a woman writing a book about something I'm deeply passionate about.

I'm still learning every single day.

What I do have is thousands of hours of research, years of investing, countless conversations with brilliant minds, and an unwavering conviction about where I see the future of finance heading.

With complete confidence, I can tell you what I have chosen to do with my own money.

I have planted my seeds.

I continue to water them and I am learning (painfully) how to remain PATIENT.

And I continue to increase my position because, in my heart and soul, I know these are among the most extraordinary generational wealth opportunities of our lifetime.

Could I be wrong?

Of course.

Every investment carries risk, and no one can predict the future with absolute certainty.

Yet conviction isn't built on certainty. Conviction is built on study, experience, discernment, and the courage to act when your research aligns with your intuition.

My hope is that this book becomes the beginning of your journey.

Because the greatest investment you will ever make isn't into XRP or any other digital asset.

It's into your own financial education.

Once no one can take that from you, you've already begun creating generational wealth.

Sometimes the greatest returns don't come from finding the perfect investment. They come from having the patience to stay planted while everyone else is walking away.

Summary of reasons I LOVE XRP:

1. It has one of the clearest regulatory positions among major digital assets in the U.S.

2. It has achieved significant legal victories regarding its regulatory status.

3. It's faster, cheaper, and more energy-efficient than BTC and ETH.

4. Transactions settle quickly with minimal costs.

5. The XRP Ledger has maintained a strong security track record.

6. The user experience is simple and intuitive, with wallets like XUMM offering a seamless experience.

7. XRP is built for efficient cross-border payments.

8. Ripple has established partnerships with major financial institutions and global enterprises.

9. It offers a real-world utility that continues to drive adoption.

10. Ripple has assembled a strong team and secured major courtroom wins against the SEC.

11. Ripple is widely recognized for its commitment to transparency.

12. The XRP Ledger operates on a decentralized validator network.

13. XRP is still trading below its previous all-time high of around $3.70.

14. Growing liquidity and increasing institutional interest could become major catalysts.

15. Some investors are rotating from ETH into XRP amid ongoing debates surrounding Ethereum's early history.

16. With uncertainty in traditional markets, some investors are turning to digital assets as an alternative.

17. The XRP community remains one of the most passionate, active, and resilient communities in crypto.

The future looks bright, and I believe XRP is just getting started.

Need I say more…. It's Coming!

CHAPTER 8

Planting the Habit

"Small, smart choices, consistently over time, lead to radical differences."

— Darren Hardy

Planting a seed is a single decision.

Growing a garden is a series of decisions repeated over and over again.

It's very easy to get excited when prices are rising, yet when prices fall people become discouraged and they stop planting because you can't see what's happening beneath the surface.

We look for instant gratification. Look bigger!

Every magnificent oak tree began as a tiny seed that spent months growing roots before anyone could see evidence of its progress.

Investing follows the same principle. The roots are growing long before the harvest arrives.

This is why I love dollar cost averaging.

Dollar cost averaging, often called DCA, is one of the simplest investing strategies you'll ever learn.

Instead of trying to predict the perfect day to invest, you commit to investing a consistent amount on a consistent schedule. Some days you'll buy when prices are higher. Other days you'll buy when prices are lower. Over time, your purchases average out, removing much of the emotion and guesswork that causes so many investors to make poor decisions.

For me, dollar cost averaging is about much more than buying an asset.

It's keeping a promise to my future self.

Every purchase is another seed planted in my Golden Garden. I don't plant based on fear. I don't plant based on excitement. I plant because I have a plan.

One of the greatest gifts you can give yourself as an investor is a long-term perspective.

The market will have exciting seasons and difficult seasons. There will always be headlines trying to convince you that you should buy today or sell tomorrow. If your decisions are driven by emotion, you'll constantly be digging up the very seeds you're trying to grow.

Instead, keep your eyes on the harvest.

Know your freedom number. Your freedom number is the amount of money you need to live off the interest, never disrupting the Golden Seed that continues to provide fruit year over year.

Take time to define what financial freedom actually looks like for you.

How much monthly income would allow you to live the life you dream about?

What experiences do you want to create?

How do you want to serve your family, your community, and the people God has placed in your life?

Maybe it's $2M, $5M, $10M, $100M or $1 billion whatever it is, do the math and visualize that number. Call it in!

When your vision is clear, today's market fluctuations become much less important. You stop reacting to every headline because you know where you're going. Your daily actions become connected to a much bigger purpose.

Every time you dollar cost average, remind yourself that you are voting for your future.

You are choosing discipline over emotion, consistency over perfection, and stewardship over speculation.

Wealth is rarely created by one brilliant decision.

More often, it is created by thousands of ordinary decisions made with extraordinary consistency.

Keep planting.

Your future harvest is depending on the seeds you choose to plant today.

I ask: What small amount can you commit to adding to your garden daily, weekly, monthly, bi-monthly, semi-annually or randomly.

CHAPTER 9

Planting Your First Seed

"The best time to plant a tree was 20 years ago. The second best time is now."

— Chinese Proverb

By now, you understand what cryptocurrency is, why I believe digital assets deserve a place in a diversified portfolio, and why XRP became one of the core seeds in my own Golden Garden.

Now it's time to plant your first seed.

If you've never purchased cryptocurrency before, I know this part can feel intimidating. The good news is that buying digital assets today is much easier than it was when I first started. The apps are more user-friendly, the educational resources are better, and the process has become much more straightforward.

Let's walk through it together.

Step 1: Choose an Exchange

Think of a cryptocurrency exchange as an online brokerage account. Just as you would use a brokerage to purchase stocks, you'll use a cryptocurrency exchange to purchase digital assets.

The two exchanges I personally use most often are Coinbase and Kraken. Both are well-established, easy to navigate, and available to U.S. customers.

Download either the Coinbase or Kraken app from the Apple App Store or Google Play Store and create your account directly from your phone. I recommend using the mobile app because it makes buying, tracking, and managing your digital assets simple and convenient.

I've also included referral links in the back of this book.

When you use those links to create your account, you'll receive bonus cryptocurrency as part of the exchange's referral program. Once it's credited to your account, you can swap it for XRP or any other digital asset you choose.

Step 2: Create Your Account

Once you've downloaded the app, you'll create an account using your email address and a secure password.

Bccause cryptocurrency exchanges operate under financial regulations, you'll also be asked to verify your identity. This process is called Know Your Customer, or KYC.

You'll typically provide:

• Your legal name

• Your date of birth

• Your address

• A government-issued photo ID

Some exchanges may also ask you to take a selfie to confirm your identity.

This verification process helps protect your account and is a normal part of opening any financial account.

Step 3: Secure Your Account

Before depositing any money, take a few minutes to strengthen your security.

Create a unique password.

Enable two-factor authentication.

Save your recovery information in a secure location.

These simple steps can dramatically reduce the risk of unauthorized access.

Step 4: Connect Your Bank Account

Next, you'll link your checking account or debit card. I do not recommend using a credit card.

Most exchanges will walk you through this process step by step.

Once connected, you'll be able to transfer U.S. dollars into your exchange account.

Step 5: Purchase Your First Digital Asset

After your funds are available, tap the search bar and type the name or ticker symbol of the asset you'd like to purchase.

For example:

XRP

XLM

HBAR

XDC (Not on Coinbase, use Kraken or Uphold)

Choose the amount you'd like to invest.

Many exchanges allow you to start with as little as $10 or $20.

Review the transaction carefully before selecting Buy. Pressing the buttons, you are now an INVESTOR!

Congratulations.

You've officially planted your first seed.

Step 6: Consider Automatic Investing

One of my favorite features on most exchanges is recurring purchases.

As discussed above, Dollar Cost Averaging, or DCA, and it's one of the strategies I personally use.

Instead of deciding on the perfect day to invest, you can schedule automatic purchases daily, weekly, or monthly.

Automation removes much of the emotion from investing and helps you remain consistent over time.

A Few Final Thoughts

The first purchase is almost always the hardest.

After that, the process becomes familiar.

Remember, you don't need thousands of dollars to begin.

You simply need to begin.

One seed planted today has the potential to grow into something extraordinary tomorrow.

Every experienced investor was once a beginner.

Today is simply your first step.

Your First Crypto Checklist

☐ Download Coinbase or Kraken

☐ Verify your identity

☐ Enable two-factor authentication

☐ Connect your bank account

☐ Deposit funds

☐ Purchase your first digital asset

☐ Set up an automatic Dollar Cost Averaging plan

☐ Celebrate planting your first seed 🌱

CHAPTER 10

How Much to Plant?

"Little by little, a little becomes a lot."

— Tanzanian Proverb

This is probably the number one question I get. My answer is always the same.

Invest an amount that allows you to stay in the game.

If you invest so much that every market dip keeps you awake at night, you've planted more than your emotions are ready to handle.

If you invest so little that you never build meaningful ownership, your garden may take much longer to flourish.

There is a sweet spot.

I encourage people to begin with an amount they can consistently invest month after month, regardless of what the market is doing. Wealth is rarely created by one giant purchase. More often, it's created through consistent planting over time.

The market will rise.

The market will fall.

Your job is simply to continue planting.

One rule I never break is this:

Never invest money you can't afford to leave invested for the long term.

By long term I mean 2030. 3.5years from the time of this writing.

If there's a chance you'll need that money next month, next year, or even in the next few years, it probably shouldn't be invested. Great investments often reward patience, not urgency.

Charlie Munger once said:

> *"The big money is not in the buying and the selling, but in the waiting."*

Those words perfectly capture my investing philosophy.

As I'm writing this book, XRP's all-time high is approximately **$3.70**, while today it's currently trading around **$1.11**. Personally, I see that as an excellent buying opportunity.

If I had additional cash that I didn't need for a few years, I would be comfortable making a larger purchase today and then continuing to dollar-cost average over time.

Whether you choose to invest a lump sum, dollar-cost average, or combine the two, the most important thing is to have a plan and stick to it.

Remember, investing isn't about finding the perfect day to buy.

It's about owning great assets and giving them the time they need to grow.

My personal Strategy: Tip Yourself First

Before I became an investor, I was a bartender for many years.

My livelihood once depended on the generosity of other people's tips. As a bartender, I learned to appreciate every dollar someone left behind. Naturally, I became a generous tipper myself.

Today, I apply that same principle to every dollar I earn.

Before I pay anyone else, I tip myself.

Whenever money comes in, I automatically set aside 20% to invest in my future.

It's my way of making sure the first person rewarded for my hard work is me.

Most people pay their bills first, spend what's left, and hope there's something remaining to invest.

I do the opposite.

I pay my future first.

Then I figure out how to live on the rest.

You don't have to use 20%. Start with whatever percentage you can consistently commit to. The important part is making yourself the first person you pay every time money comes into your life.

Your future self has been working for you every single day.

It's time to start tipping them.

Below is a snapshot of current XRP wallet distribution and the percentage of holders each milestone represents.

Personally, I think reaching **2,500 XRP** is an excellent long-term goal because it places you among the top 10% of XRP wallets based on today's distribution.

Whether your goal is **100 XRP, 500 XRP, 2,500 XRP, or beyond**, the most important thing is to build your position consistently and at a pace that fits your financial situation.

Your future wealth won't be determined by one big purchase.

It will be determined by the habits you repeat year after year.

Percentage of accounts with balance starting at...

Percentage	# Accounts	Balance equals (or greater than)
0.01 %	657	5,730,534.747573 XRP
0.1 %	6,570	370,734.215954 XRP
0.2 %	13,140	200,314.089508 XRP
0.5 %	32,849	100,000.326609 XRP
1 %	65,698	50,763.023455 XRP
2 %	131,396	25,767.636266 XRP
3 %	197,094	16,348.594367 XRP
4 %	262,792	11,043.421102 XRP
5 %	328,490	8,762.755368 XRP
10 %	656,981	2,480.017463 XRP

Here's a good way to measure:

Seedling — **0–500 XRP**

Sprout — **500–2,500 XRP**

🌿 Growing Garden — **2,500–10,000 XRP**

🌳 Thriving Garden — **10,000–50,000 XRP**

🏛️ Legacy Garden — **50,000+ XRP**

As always, you do what's best for you.

Chapter Reflection

Every generation experiences a moment when technology reshapes the world.

Railroads connected continents.

Electricity transformed cities.

The internet changed how we communicate, learn, shop, and build businesses.

Today, blockchain technology is beginning to reshape how value moves around the world, how assets are owned, and how financial systems connect.

We're also witnessing an important shift in regulation. In the United States, lawmakers are working toward a clearer legal framework for digital assets through legislation such as the

CLARITY Act. At the time of writing, the bill has advanced significantly and is moving through the legislative process, bringing the industry closer to the regulatory clarity that many institutions have been waiting for. While it has not yet become law, its progress reflects how seriously digital assets are now being considered at the highest levels.

History has shown that the greatest opportunities often exist while they still look unfamiliar.

By the time everyone agrees on the opportunity, the biggest advantages of being early have often diminished. Institutions have begun building, innovation has accelerated, and participation has become far more competitive.

That doesn't mean anyone can predict the future. It means preparation has value.

That's why education matters.

That's why consistency matters.

That's why planting matters.

Take a moment to reflect.

- What opportunities are you preparing yourself to recognize?

- What knowledge will you commit to gaining over the next year?
- What seed can you begin planting today?
- What future are you intentionally cultivating for yourself and your family?

Remember, every thriving garden begins with a single seed.

One decision.

One investment.

One habit.

One courageous first step.

My hope is that years from now you'll look back on this season with gratitude—not because you knew exactly what would happen, but because you chose to learn, prepare, and participate while the garden was still being planted.

Your Golden Garden is waiting.

Now it's time to plant your first seed.

PART III

PROTECT

PART III: PROTECT

Wisdom from Proverbs

"The prudent see danger and take refuge, but the simple keep going and pay the penalty."
— Proverbs 22:3

King Solomon understood that wisdom isn't only about creating wealth. It's also about protecting it.

A wise farmer doesn't wait until the storm is on the horizon before repairing the fence. He doesn't wait until animals begin eating his crops before building a gate. He prepares in advance because he knows that every healthy harvest deserves to be protected.

Preparation isn't driven by fear.

It's driven by wisdom.

The same principle applies to your financial life.

Building wealth takes years of patience, discipline, and faithful planting. Yet a single careless decision can undo what took decades to build. Throughout history, fortunes have been lost, not because they weren't earned, but because they weren't protected.

This section of the book is about becoming a wise steward of the wealth you're creating.

You'll learn how to safely store your digital assets, create a protection plan for your family, guard your privacy, recognize scams before they become costly mistakes, and build habits that help preserve your wealth for generations to come.

Just as a farmer protects his fields so they can continue producing year after year, you have a responsibility to protect the financial garden you're cultivating.

As you read the chapters ahead, remember Solomon's words. Wise people prepare before danger arrives. They understand that protection is not an act of fear. It's an act of stewardship.

Because a harvest that is carefully protected has the opportunity to bless generations.

CHAPTER 11

Rule #1: Build the Fence

"The first rule of investment is don't lose money. The second rule is never forget the first rule."

— Warren Buffett

Protect Rule #1: Build the Fence

You've prepared the soil.

You've planted the seeds.

Now it's time to build the fence.

Every thriving garden has one thing in common. Someone cared enough to protect it.

A fence isn't built because the gardener expects something bad to happen. It's built because the garden is valuable.

Your wealth deserves the same level of care.

The moment your investments begin to grow, your responsibility changes. You're no longer focused only on creating wealth. You're becoming a steward of it.

Stewardship is one of my favorite words because it reminds me that everything we have is a gift entrusted to us for a season. Our role is to care for it wisely, help it grow, and use it to bless the lives of others.

In the world of digital assets, building your fence begins with understanding if you don't protect your assets, someone else may take them.

Unlike a traditional bank account, cryptocurrency gives you the opportunity to become your own bank. That freedom is one of the greatest advantages of digital assets. It also comes with greater responsibility.

You've probably heard the phrase, **"Not your keys, not your crypto."**

When your digital assets remain on an exchange, the exchange holds the private keys that control those assets. While reputable exchanges invest heavily in security, they are still centralized companies with their own risks. These exchanges are businesses and they can go out of business or shut down. IF/when that happens, you LOSE your investment.

You MUST move your investments, your digital assets, your XRP Off of Coinbase/Kraken/Uphold/Gemini, whatever you are using.

To move you use what's called "Cold Storage" - this allows you to take custody of your own private keys. Think of it like moving cash from someone else's safe into one that you personally own and control.

Self-Custody.

Throughout this chapter, I'll show you how to build your fence one board at a time. We'll talk about cold wallets, seed phrases, common scams, passwords, two-factor authentication, and the simple habits that can help protect your Golden Garden for years to come.

Because planting the seed begins your journey.

Protecting the seed helps ensure it has the opportunity to flourish.

Cold Storage Wallet

There are several excellent cold wallets available today, including Ledger, Trezor, D'CENT, and Tangem. After trying different options and doing my own research, I personally chose Tangem because of its simplicity. I wanted something that was secure, easy to use, and beginner-friendly.

A cold wallet doesn't actually hold your cryptocurrency.

Your digital assets always remain on the blockchain. Your wallet simply protects the private keys that give you access to them. Think of your wallet as the key to your safety deposit box, not the box itself.

Why I Chose Tangem

Tangem works differently from many traditional hardware wallets. Instead of plugging a device into your computer with cables and buttons, Tangem uses secure cards that communicate with your phone by simply tapping them together.

The setup is quick, the app is intuitive, and I found it much less intimidating than some of the older hardware wallets.

One thing I especially appreciate is that Tangem provides three identical backup cards. Each card opens the same wallet, which means if one card is lost or damaged, you still have two backups.

You order Tangem directly from the company not Amazon. I have a link with 10% discount in the book resources at the back.

PRO TIP

I recommend ordering **two Tangem wallets**.

As a precaution for unknown future risks, including the continued evolution of technology such as quantum computing, I personally keep my XRP in its own dedicated wallet and store my other digital assets (alt coins example: XLM, HBAR, XDC) in a separate wallet.

XRP is my highest-conviction, long-term investment, so I prefer giving it its own vault. Keeping it separate also makes my portfolio easier to organize and reduces the likelihood of accidentally moving or managing my core holdings while working with other assets.

This isn't a requirement. It's simply the system that gives me the greatest peace of mind and has worked well for me.

This wallet makes your investment safe! Unhackable and Protected. It's absolutely vital, if you're investing in Digital Assets, primary XRP. Get the wallet and keep it safe.

Setting Up Your Wallet

When your Tangem wallet arrives, download the Tangem app from the Apple App Store or Google Play Store.

Open the app and follow the guided setup. The app will walk you through activating each card by tapping it to the back of your phone.

Take your time during this process. There is no need to rush.

Once your wallet is created, you'll be ready to receive cryptocurrency from your exchange.

Should You Use a Seed Phrase?

Tangem allows you to choose whether you want to create your wallet with a seed phrase or without one.

A seed phrase is a series of words that acts as the master backup for your wallet.

Think of it as the master key to your vault.

Anyone who has those words has the ability to recreate your wallet and access your digital assets.

That's why protecting your seed phrase is one of the most important responsibilities you'll have as a crypto investor.

Personally, I prefer using a seed phrase because I like having an additional layer of recovery beyond my backup cards. Other people prefer the simplicity of Tangem's seedless option. Neither approach is automatically better. The important thing is understanding how each one works before deciding which fits your comfort level.

Protecting Your Seed Phrase

If you choose to use a seed phrase, write it down by hand as you create your wallet.

Store it somewhere safe.

Never save it in your Notes app.

Never email it to yourself.

Never take a picture of it.

Never upload it to cloud storage.

Never type it into a website or share it with anyone claiming they need it.

No legitimate company, customer support representative, or investment professional will ever ask for your seed phrase.

If someone asks for it, it's a scam.

Treat your seed phrase the same way you would treat the deed to your home or the combination to your vault.

It deserves that level of protection.

CHAPTER 12

Rule #2: Protecting Your Legacy

"The greatest use of life is to spend it for something that will outlast it."

— William James

One of the greatest advantages of owning digital assets is true ownership.

For the first time in history, everyday people have the ability to become their own bank. You control your assets, your private keys, and your financial future. No bank can freeze your account. No institution stands between you and your wealth.

That level of freedom is extraordinary.

It also comes with extraordinary responsibility.

Unlike a traditional bank account, digital assets don't automatically transfer to your loved ones. There isn't a customer service number to call if no one knows where your wallet is or how to access it. If your private keys are lost, your digital assets could be inaccessible forever.

Take a moment and ask yourself this question:

If you were unexpectedly hit by a bus tomorrow, would your family know how to access your digital assets?

Would they know where your cold wallet is?

Would they know where your backup cards or recovery information are stored?

Would they know which assets you own, your long-term investment strategy, or whether you intended to hold or sell them?

If the answer is no, today is the perfect day to create a plan.

Choose someone you trust completely. It might be your spouse, an adult child, another family member, a trusted friend, your attorney, or the executor of your estate.

Then create clear, written instructions that include:

- Where your cold storage wallets are located.
- Where your backup cards or recovery information are securely stored.
- How to access your digital assets.

- Which assets you own.
- Who should inherit them?
- Any instructions regarding when or how you would like those assets distributed or sold.

Store this information in a secure place, and make sure the person you trust most knows how to access it if the unexpected happens.

Planning ahead is one of the greatest acts of love you can offer your family.

Building wealth requires vision, discipline, and patience. Protecting it requires the same level of intention.

Your digital assets represent years of learning, sacrifice, and faithful investing. Taking the time to organize your accounts, document your wishes, and name the right beneficiaries helps ensure that everything you've worked so hard to build remains available to the people you love.

Your legacy deserves more than good intentions. It deserves a clear plan.

One day, your family will be grateful that you took the time to prepare today.

Because the greatest legacy isn't simply the wealth you create.

It's the wisdom, preparation, and opportunity you leave behind.

CHAPTER 13

Rule #3: Zip Your Mouth

"Whoever guards his mouth preserves his life."

— Proverbs 13:3

One of the best ways to protect your wealth costs absolutely nothing.

Keep your mouth shut.

As your portfolio grows, it can be tempting to celebrate your wins, post screenshots, or tell friends and family how much you've made.

Don't.

Nothing good comes from advertising your wealth.

The single biggest mistake you can make is telling people how much XRP or cryptocurrency you own.

Never disclose your holdings.

Treat that information the same way you would treat your bank account balance, your Social Security number, or the combination to your home safe.

It's private.

It's confidential.

It's nobody's business but yours.

The fewer people who know what you own, the lower your risk of becoming a target for scams, phishing attempts, theft, or unwanted attention.

Celebrate your success quietly.

Let your lifestyle speak for itself.

Real wealth doesn't need an audience.

Remember, in the world of digital assets, privacy is security.

The less people know about your holdings, the better protected you are.

Loose lips sink ships.

Make it a habit to stay humble, stay private, and stay secure.

CHAPTER 14

Rule #4: Scammers

"Trust, but verify."

— Ronald Reagan

You've worked hard to build your portfolio.

Don't let someone else steal it.

Unfortunately, as digital assets become more valuable, scammers become more creative. They're constantly inventing new ways to separate people from their money, and they're incredibly good at making their scams look legitimate.

Over the years I've learned one simple truth:

Scammers don't hack wallets. They hack people.

They use fear.

They use greed.

They use urgency.

They use excitement.

And if they can get you to stop thinking for just a few seconds, they've won.

One of the oldest tricks is offering something for nothing.

You'll receive emails telling you that you've won free XRP. You'll see advertisements for giveaways, airdrops, exclusive investment opportunities, or programs claiming they'll double your XRP if you send them a small amount first.

They're all designed to do one thing.

Separate you from your money.

If it sounds too good to be true, it almost always is.

Another common scam is phishing emails. These emails often look identical to messages from your exchange, wallet provider, or another company you trust. They may tell you there's suspicious activity on your account or that you need to verify your wallet immediately.

Don't click the link.

Instead, close the email and go directly to the company's official website by typing the address yourself or using a bookmark you've already saved.

One wrong click can change your life.

You'll also receive random messages on social media from people claiming to be investment experts, customer support representatives, or successful traders who want to help you make money.

Ignore them.

Legitimate companies don't contact customers through unsolicited direct messages, and no honest investor is searching the internet for strangers to make wealthy.

Perhaps the most important rule of all is this:

Never give anyone your seed phrase or recovery phrase.

Not customer support.

Not your wallet provider.

Not a friend.

Not a family member.

No legitimate company will ever ask for it.

Anyone who has your recovery phrase has complete control of your digital assets.

A close friend of mine learned a painful lesson about trust. He invested more than **$250,000** of his family's money into what appeared to be a professional investment company. Everything looked legitimate. The presentations were polished, the people were convincing, and the promised returns sounded reasonable.

Until one day the company disappeared.

So did every dollar.

Watching that happen reinforced something I'll never forget.

No one will ever care about your money more than you do.

That's why I prefer to stay in control of my own assets. I make my own decisions. I hold my own keys. I don't hand my financial future to someone else simply because they sound confident.

Whenever someone pressures you to "act now," take that as your cue to slow down.

Real investment opportunities don't disappear because you took five minutes to think.

Scams often do.

If you ever feel uncertain, stop.

Do your research.

Ask questions.

Sleep on it.

Your money will still be there tomorrow.

The opportunity worth taking usually will be too.

Remember, building wealth takes years.

Losing it can happen in a single click.

Protect your XRP.

Protect your private keys.

Protect your future.

Because in the world of digital assets, security isn't optional.

It's part of being a successful investor.

CHAPTER 15

Rule #5: Gifting

Once you've become a savvy investor and truly understand the value of this asset, it's only natural to want the people you love to benefit from it too. Whether it's your children, grandchildren, family, or close friends, you'll probably feel an overwhelming desire to help them experience the same opportunity you've discovered.

I encourage you to share your knowledge with them. Tell them why you invested. Share this book. Encourage them to do their own research, ask questions, and develop their own conviction. If they decide to invest because they understand the opportunity, they'll appreciate what they own far more than if it was simply handed to them.

What I would caution against is buying the investment for them and giving it to them as a gift.

That advice may seem surprising, especially after spending an entire book explaining why I believe so strongly in this investment. However, my reasoning has very little to do with the investment itself and everything to do with human behavior.

You didn't become a savvy investor overnight.

You earned it.

You spent time learning. You researched the opportunity. You questioned what you thought you knew. You developed confidence in your decision. You learned to ignore the daily noise and focus on the long-term picture.

That process created something far more valuable than the investment itself.

It created conviction.

Conviction cannot be gifted.

If you buy this investment for someone else, they receive the asset, but they never experienced the journey that gave you confidence to hold it. Without that understanding, the investment is simply money sitting in an account waiting to be spent.

Now imagine what happens if, just a few months after you give it to them, the price rises like an elevator.

It increases tenfold.

Suddenly, they're looking at more money than they've ever had in their entire life.

For you, it's exciting because you understand what that appreciation could mean over the next ten or twenty years.

For them, it's something completely different.

That money starts burning a hole in their wallet.

They begin thinking about everything they could buy with it. Maybe it's a flashy car that starts losing value the moment they drive it off the lot. Maybe it's a luxury vacation they've always dreamed about. Maybe it's designer clothes, expensive gadgets, or something else that feels exciting in the moment.

So they sell.

From their perspective, it makes perfect sense.

They didn't work for that money.

It feels like free money.

Why not enjoy it?

What they don't realize is that they haven't traded an investment for a vacation.

They may have traded a lifetime of financial freedom for one week on a beach.

That vacation will eventually become a memory.

That car will eventually wear out.

The money will be gone.

But the investment could have continued growing. It could have produced income for decades. It could have funded vacations every year instead of just one. It could have helped pay for homes, college educations, retirement, businesses, and opportunities for generations to come.

They see instant dollars.

You see long-term wealth.

They see something to spend.

You see something that can continue creating wealth long after today's excitement has faded.

The difference isn't intelligence.

The difference is perspective.

You understand the value because you've taken the time to become a savvy investor.

They haven't.

That's why I believe you're better off keeping ownership of the investment yourself.

Allow it to continue growing. Let it continue doing what you purchased it to do.

When the time is right, you can decide how to share the wealth it creates.

You can help them buy their first home.

You can help pay for college.

You can cover unexpected medical expenses.

You can take the entire family on that dream vacation.

You can gift cash from the profits whenever you choose.

But by keeping the investment alive, you preserve the engine that continues creating wealth.

I like to think of it this way.

Imagine owning the goose that lays golden eggs.

If you become impatient and kill the goose, you might enjoy one large meal today, but you'll never receive another golden egg.

The wiser choice is to protect the goose.

Collect the golden eggs.

Share the golden eggs with the people you love.

But keep the goose alive.

Your investment is that goose.

Protect it.

Let it continue producing wealth.

Then use that wealth to bless your family for years, even decades, to come.

The greatest gift you can give your children and grandchildren isn't an investment they don't yet understand.

It's the knowledge to become savvy investors themselves, combined with the financial freedom that comes from preserving the investment instead of spending it the first time it creates life-changing wealth.

Chapter Reflection

The strongest security system you'll ever have is wisdom.

Technology will continue to evolve. Scammers will continue searching for new ways to deceive people. Every new innovation creates new opportunities, and it also creates new responsibilities.

Fortunately, one thing never changes.

Knowledge remains your greatest protection.

Every time you slow down, verify information, question extraordinary claims, and refuse to let emotion make your decisions, you're strengthening the fence around your Golden Garden.

Remember, scammers succeed by creating urgency. Wise investors create space to think.

Take a moment to reflect.

- Have you learned how to recognize the warning signs of a scam?
- Would you pause before clicking an unexpected link or responding to an unsolicited message?
- Have you committed to protecting your seed phrase as carefully as your greatest financial asset?
- Who can you turn to for trusted guidance when something doesn't feel right?

Building wealth is a journey of patience.

Protecting wealth is a practice of wisdom.

Every careful decision strengthens the foundation you've worked so hard to build and helps preserve the harvest you're creating for yourself and the people you love.

Your Golden Garden continues to grow because you've chosen to plant with intention, protect with wisdom, and move forward with confidence.

That's how lasting wealth is cultivated.

PART IV

PROSPER

PART IV: PROSPER

Wisdom from Proverbs

"A generous person will prosper; whoever refreshes others will be refreshed."
— Proverbs 11:25

King Solomon reminds us that prosperity was never meant to stop with us. It was always meant to create something bigger than ourselves.

Throughout this book, we've prepared the soil, planted the seeds, and protected the harvest. Now it's time to enjoy the rewards of that patience and discipline.

Prosperity isn't about chasing the biggest bank account.

It's about creating choices.

It's about having the freedom to live life on your terms, take care of the people you love, continue building wealth, and leave the world better than you found it.

Money is simply a tool.

When it's used wisely, it can create freedom for your family, open doors for future generations, fund dreams, grow businesses, support meaningful causes, and create opportunities that once seemed impossible.

This final section is all about making your harvest count.

I'll share the exit strategy I've designed, how I plan to transform one successful investment into a lifetime of wealth, why I continue planting even after I've harvested, and where I see the future headed.

The goal isn't simply to make money.

The goal is to make money work for you.

To build assets that continue producing income.

To create opportunities instead of obligations.

And to leave something meaningful behind for the people you love.

One day, someone else's life may be better because of the decisions you're making today.

That's the true meaning of prosperity.

Let's discover how to make your harvest last for generations.

CHAPTER 16

Exit Strategy

"Rule No. 1: Never lose money. Rule No. 2: Never forget Rule No. 1."

— Warren Buffett

If you've made it this far, congratulations!

You've done the hard part. You've prepared your mind, planted your seeds, stayed consistent through the ups and downs, and learned how to protect your digital wealth. Now it's time to talk about the harvest.

This is the chapter I've been looking forward to the most because this is where all of your patience, discipline, and consistency begin to pay off. We'll build a strategy for turning paper profits into real wealth, and then we'll have a little fun by exploring some hypothetical price predictions. They're simply thought exercises to help you dream a little bigger and imagine what's possible. They aren't promises, guarantees, or financial advice.

Believe it or not, taking profits is one of the hardest parts of investing. Most people spend years asking, "What should I buy?" Very few spend any time asking, "What am I going to do when my investment actually takes off?"

The truth is, if you don't decide how you'll harvest your profits before the market becomes emotional, there's a good chance you'll make emotional decisions when the time comes.

That's how fortunes are built.

It's also how fortunes disappear.

Greed Is Expensive

Every bull market follows the same familiar pattern. Prices begin climbing, excitement builds, and suddenly everyone is talking about cryptocurrency.

Friends and family who never cared before start asking what they should buy. The media jumps on board, social media fills with predictions that every coin is headed "to the moon," and it feels like the party will never end. It’s happening right now too. STAY STOIC.

As prices continue climbing, greed quietly replaces logic. Instead of celebrating the incredible gains they've already made, investors start wondering if they can squeeze out just a little more. They convince themselves they'll know exactly when it's time to sell.

The problem is, almost nobody does.

Markets don't ring a bell at the top. By the time everyone realizes the bull market has ended, prices have often fallen dramatically. Investors who were celebrating life-changing gains only weeks before suddenly find themselves watching much of their wealth disappear because they never created a plan to harvest it.

Learn From My Mistake

I know this because I've lived it…recently.

I watched my portfolio grow faster than I ever imagined. Every day seemed better than the last, and I became convinced the market would keep climbing. I hadn't taken the time to write down an exit strategy because I honestly thought I'd just know when it was time to sell.

I was wrong.

I kept telling myself, "Just a little higher," believing I'd recognize the perfect moment. Instead, the market turned, and I watched a significant portion of my gains disappear.

That experience humbled me; it also taught me one of the most valuable lessons of my investing journey. Buying is only half the equation. If you want to build lasting wealth, you also need to know how you're going to harvest it.

You Don't Have to Sell Everything

At one point, I thought there were only two choices. You either sold everything, or you held on and hoped the market kept climbing.

Then I realized there was another option.

I could take profits gradually while allowing the rest of my investment to continue growing. I stopped trying to predict the perfect top and started following a strategy I could stick with.

That gave me confidence because I knew exactly what I was going to do before the market tried to convince me otherwise.

My Harvest Strategy

People ask me all the time what my exit strategy looks like, and I'm always happy to share it.

This isn't financial advice. It's simply the strategy I've created based on my own goals, convictions, and risk tolerance.

One thing I've learned is that nobody consistently times the market perfectly. Rather than trying to predict the exact top, I decided to create a written plan and trust it.

I use what's called a **Ladder Exit Strategy**.

As my investment reaches the price milestones I've chosen in advance, I sell 10% of my active holdings at each level. The decisions have already been made, so when the market becomes emotional, I simply follow the plan.

I love this approach because every milestone is a reason to celebrate. I lock in a portion of my profits, pay myself for staying disciplined, and still have the majority of my investment working for me if prices continue climbing.

That gives me incredible peace of mind because I know I'm building wealth intentionally instead of reacting emotionally.

There Is No Perfect Top

Nobody consistently sells at the exact top of the market, and that's perfectly okay.

I've made peace with that. What you'll find is the exact opposite happens of what you anticipate, be ok with it.

If I capture most of a bull market, I'm thrilled. Someone else can have the last few percentage points. I'm not trying to win a trophy for calling the perfect top. I'm building wealth that creates freedom for my family, opens new opportunities, and allows me to continue investing for years to come.

Remember Why You Started

As your portfolio grows, keep asking yourself one simple question:

What is this money going to do for my life?

Maybe it's paying off your home. Maybe it's becoming debt-free, traveling the world, starting a business, helping your children, supporting your church, creating a Foundation and/or creating a legacy that lasts for generations.

Your answer is your **why**.

Money without purpose has a way of disappearing. Money connected to purpose creates freedom, opportunity, and lasting impact. Every dollar you harvest should move you one step closer to the life you imagined when you planted your very first seed.

Celebrate the Harvest

When your investments begin producing fruit, take time to celebrate.

Seriously... CELEBRATE!

Take the vacation. Enjoy a special dinner with your spouse. Buy something meaningful. Make memories you'll still be talking about years from now.

Then pause for a moment and appreciate what you've accomplished. Celebrate your discipline, your patience, and your willingness to stay the course while so many others gave up.

Always remember that the purpose of investing isn't simply to make more money. The purpose is to create more life. More freedom. More time with the people you love. More opportunities to learn, grow, give generously, and pursue the dreams God has placed on your heart.

To me, that's the true harvest.

Here's my strategy, decide on your trigger exit points. Then when you do take profits, reinvest them! I love ETF's

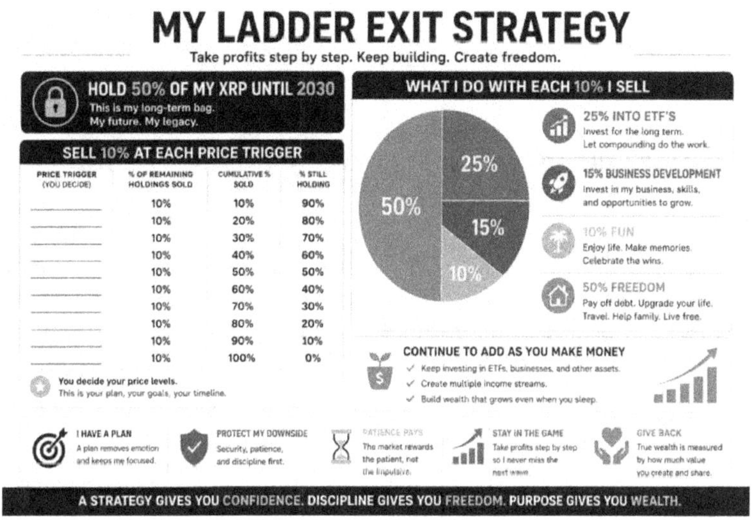

CHAPTER 17

Continue the Growth

"An investment in knowledge pays the best interest."

— Benjamin Franklin

Turning One Investment into a Lifetime of Wealth

I love asking myself…

"What are you going to do after you start taking profits?"

My answer is always the same.

I'm putting my money right back to work.

Every dollar has a purpose. Instead of sitting idle, I want my money growing, producing, and creating new opportunities for my future. Just as a gardener plants seeds from one harvest to produce the next, I believe each financial success should become the foundation for the one that follows.

That's where ETFs come in.

What Is an ETF?

ETF stands for **Exchange-Traded Fund.**

The name may sound complicated, but the idea is surprisingly simple.

Imagine walking through a large orchard instead of planting a single apple tree. Rather than depending on one tree to produce fruit, you own a small piece of the entire orchard. If one tree has a poor season, hundreds of others continue to grow and produce.

That's how an ETF works.

Instead of investing in a single company, an ETF allows you to own small pieces of many companies through one investment. Think of it as a basket filled with businesses. Some ETFs hold hundreds of companies, giving you broad diversification with a single purchase.

Investing in the Stock Market

Unlike cryptocurrency, ETFs are bought and sold on the stock market through a brokerage account.

The beauty of ETFs is that you don't have to become an expert at picking individual stocks. Many already include some of the strongest and most successful companies in the world, allowing your investment to grow alongside them over time.

Building Long-Term Wealth

One of the reasons I love ETFs is that they can also be purchased inside retirement accounts, such as an IRA or 401(k). Depending on your personal situation and where you live, these accounts may provide valuable tax advantages while helping you build wealth for the future.

Imagine taking profits from one successful investment, placing a portion into long-term investments, and allowing those dollars to continue growing for the next twenty or thirty years.

That's how one harvest can plant the seeds for the next.

My Favorite Investments

These are my **top three favorite ETFs** and the ones I personally own. This isn't financial advice, just a glimpse into my own investment strategy. There are thousands of ETFs available, each with its own purpose and investment style. These three simply align with my long-term goals. Do your own research, continue learning, and choose the investments that best fit your financial plan.

Investment	Why I Like It
VOO	The foundation of my portfolio. It tracks the S&P 500, giving me ownership in 500 of America's largest and most established companies.
QQQ	Provides exposure to many of the world's leading technology and innovation companies, offering long-term growth potential.
XRPZ	The Franklin XRP Trust provides another way to gain exposure to XRP through a traditional investment vehicle, where available.

My goal has never been to harvest wealth once.

My goal is to create a garden that continues producing for the rest of my life.

Every harvest becomes an opportunity to plant again, allowing today's success to become tomorrow's abundance.

Keep Planting

Investing is a continuous cycle of growth and movement.

You plant.

You nurture.

You harvest.

Then you plant again.

When I take profits, I enjoy some of the harvest. I invest some back into my business. I buy assets that continue growing. And every paycheck I continue tipping myself first by investing for the future.

The goal is to create a life where your money keeps working long after you've stopped working for it.

Earning money without physically working for it. Passively!

XRPZ – Franklin XRP ETF

I'm not going to spend much time talking about ETFs in this book, but there is one I want you to know about because it's directly tied to XRP.

If you've read this far and you're thinking, *"I like everything I've learned about XRP, but I don't want to manage exchanges, wallets, or cold storage,"* then **XRPZ** may be worth exploring.

XRPZ is the Franklin XRP ETF. Instead of buying and storing XRP yourself, you purchase shares of the ETF through a traditional brokerage account, just like you would any other stock or fund. The ETF is designed to track the price of XRP, giving investors another way to participate in its potential growth.

One of the biggest advantages is that it can often be purchased inside retirement accounts such as an IRA or 401(k), allowing you to gain XRP exposure without leaving the traditional stock market.

Personally, I still prefer owning XRP directly because I value sovereign ownership and being in complete control of my assets. However, I recognize that direct ownership isn't for everyone, and I think XRPZ is an excellent alternative for investors who prefer the simplicity and familiarity of the stock market.

The important thing isn't how you invest.

The important thing is that you start investing.

There isn't a right or wrong choice. It simply depends on your goals, your comfort level, and how you prefer to invest.

CHAPTER 18

Predictions

"In investing, what is comfortable is rarely profitable."

— Robert Arnott

Just for Fun: A Big "What If?"

This is purely speculative.
No guarantees. No predictions. No financial advice. Just connecting some interesting dots and having a little fun imagining what *could* happen.

We're seeing a lot of potentially bullish developments lining up:

- 📈 Increased institutional involvement.
- 🏛 The DTCC continuing to modernize market infrastructure.
- ⚖ Regulatory clarity potentially improving through legislation like the CLARITY Act.

- 💰 More ETFs and institutional investment vehicles entering the market.
- 🤖 AI advancing at an incredible pace, driving demand for next-generation technology.
- 🌍 Blockchain adoption continuing to expand across finance, payments, tokenization, and real-world assets.
- 🚀 Technology evolving faster than at any point in history.

History has shown that markets can remain quiet for long periods...

...and then move suddenly.

When momentum returns, price discovery can happen much faster than most people expect.

Does that mean it *will* happen?

Absolutely not.

Nobody knows the future.

But it's certainly fascinating to watch these pieces slowly coming together.

If I had to offer an "intuition," it wouldn't be about specific prices or dates. My intuition is simply this:

We're still in the early chapters of one of the biggest technological transformations of our lifetime.

Just as the internet reshaped the world over the last 30 years, AI, blockchain, digital assets, robotics, and automation may reshape the next 30.

Whether that results in explosive price appreciation or a slower, steadier evolution, only time will tell.

So stay curious.

Stay humble.

Keep learning.

Manage your risk.

And enjoy watching history unfold.

Sometimes the biggest opportunities arrive quietly... before the world realizes they're there.

Let's walk through a few hypothetical scenarios.

Now, imagine you invested **$5,000** across the following digital assets. If they returned to their previous all-time highs, prices reached before greater legal clarity, your portfolio could grow to approximately **$20,000**, representing a gain of around **300%**.

These price levels are part of the market's history, offering a glimpse of what has already been possible. BEFORE we had any regulations, approval and usage.

I'm not going to pump up the excitement, as much as I want to.. I simply hope this example below expands your vision of what's possible.

Life-changing opportunities often reward those who prepare early, continue learning, and have the patience to let time do its work.

Example of $5K Investment

Crypto	Units	Buy Price	Invested	ATH Price	Value at ATH
XRP	2,222	$1.40	$3,110.80	$3.84	$8,532.48
XLM	5,000	$0.16	$800.00	$0.94	$4,700.00
HBAR	5,000	$0.095	$475.00	$0.57	$2,850.00
XDC	2,000	$0.032	$64.00	$0.19	$380.00
Ondo	1,663	$0.33	$550.00	$2.14	$3,558.82
	Total		**$4,999.80**		**$20,021.30**

$5,000 NOW = $20,021 LATER!

Totals

- **Total Invested: $4,999.80**
- **Total Value at Previous ATHs: $20,021.30**
- **Total Profit: $15,021.50**
- **Overall ROI: 300.44%**

To go where we've already been, with no utility.

Now Let's Get a Little Wild

Here are my personal predictions. I could be wildly right, wildly wrong, or somewhere in between, and that's what makes this so exciting. Let's see how the next few years unfold together!

Timeline Predictions

Do you research, sit with it and visualize what you personally feel could happen….

Let's see how close I get!!!

Jenny's Predictions						
Asset	**Price as of 7/15/26**	**Fall/Winter 2026**	**2027**	**2028**	**2029**	**2030**
XRP	$1.11	$111	$1,111	$5,555	$2,222	$11,111
XLM	$0.187	$2	$8	$30	$10	$300
HBAR	$0.06	$1.50	$6	$22	$8	$200
XDC	$0.02	$1	$5	$20	$9	$177
ONDO	$0.35	$5	$200	$440	$200	$1,000

What would your investment look like if something like this actually happened by 2030?

I mean seriously!!!

This is exactly why I wrote this book. I wanted to introduce you to an **opportunity** that deserves your attention before the rest of the world fully catches on and prices are too outrageous.

Getting started doesn't require thousands of dollars. **It simply requires taking the first step.**

If this moment becomes what many expect it could become, you'll be grateful you took the time to learn today instead of looking back years from now wishing you had started sooner.

If you invest only **$100 in XRP** and it went to $10K:

$100 = 93.46 XRP (at $1.07)

XRP Price (POSSIBILITY in 2030) =$10K

$100 NOW = $934,600

Crazy? Maybe.

Impossible? History says never count anything out.

Every investment comes with risk. Every life-changing opportunity has also started with people who were willing to take that risk before everyone else saw it.

One thing I know for sure is this...

You have to be in the game to win the game.

So start where you are. Start with what you can. Plant your first seed and see where it takes you.

Your future self just might thank you.

Okay... Time to land this ship because I'm overflowing with excitement.

CHAPTER 19

Becoming an Intuitive Steward

"No one has ever become poor by giving."

— Anne Frank

Close your eyes for just a moment and allow yourself to imagine that everything you've worked so patiently toward has become your reality.

Picture yourself waking up without an alarm because your time finally belongs to you. Your thoughts no longer revolve around deadlines, bills, or whether you can afford the life you've always dreamed about. Instead, you're thinking about where your family wants to explore next, what project God has placed on your heart, and whose life you might have the opportunity to bless today.

You get to be the Blessing for Others!

Imagine walking into your parents' home with the keys to the house they've always deserved. Watching tears fill their eyes as they realize the sacrifices they made for you have come full circle.

Imagine taking your children to places they once only read about in books, creating memories that become stories they tell their own children someday.

Picture yourself sitting on the porch of your dream home as the sun rises across the property. The coffee tastes a little better because it isn't rushed. The silence feels different because it isn't filled with worry. For the first time, your mind has room to dream again and bigger and bolder.

Now imagine using your resources to build something that outlives you.

Perhaps it's a business that creates meaningful careers for hundreds of families.

Perhaps it's a scholarship that helps a student become the first college graduate in their family.

Perhaps it's a children's hospital, a church, a ministry, or a foundation that quietly changes thousands of lives long after you're gone.

Whatever God has placed inside your heart, you finally have the **freedom** to pursue it without hesitation.

As you continue to picture that future, you'll probably notice something surprising. The excitement isn't coming from the money itself. It's coming from the life the money allows you to create. The greatest reward was never the account balance.

The greatest reward was becoming the kind of person who could steward it wisely.

This is where your Ikigai comes alive.

Everything you've learned about yourself, every lesson you've lived through, every gift you've been given, and every dream that's been growing in your heart now has room to flourish.

Your wealth becomes a tool that allows you to live fully in your purpose rather than postponing it for another day.

I hope you dream so big that your grandchildren's children thank you for decisions you made before they were even born.

I hope your generosity becomes part of your family culture, your courage inspires others to think differently, and your life becomes proof that extraordinary things happen when ordinary people choose faith, patience, and stewardship over fear.

When you finally reach your harvest, I hope you don't stop dreaming.

I pray for you to DREAM GREATER!

God created you with extraordinary purpose, and through Him, your life can accomplish more than you ever imagined.

Go now.

It's time to fly.

Live with courage.
Lead with wisdom.
Give with generosity.
Love without limits.

Create the life you were created to live.

Leave every person, every community, and every generation better because you were here.

Go create a better world for humanity.

The garden is yours.

Now it's time to make it flourish.

I LOVE YOU AND I'M CHEERING FOR YOU EVERY STEP OF THE WAY!

Chapter Reflection

True prosperity isn't measured by the size of your bank account. It's measured by the difference your life and your wealth make in the lives of others.

As your Golden Garden grows, remember that money is simply a tool. When stewarded with wisdom, gratitude, and generosity, it creates opportunities, strengthens families, and leaves a legacy that can impact generations.

May your harvest become more than financial success. May it become a source of hope, purpose, and blessing for everyone your life touches.

Closing Words

Wealth in the hands of good people changes the world. ~Jenny Connolley

If you've made it this far, thank you from the bottom of my heart for taking this journey with me.

When I first bought XRP back in 2017, I never could have imagined where it would lead. What started as simple curiosity became thousands of hours of research, learning, praying, asking questions, and following every breadcrumb God placed in front of me. With every answer I found, my conviction grew stronger, and eventually I realized I couldn't keep what I was learning to myself.

That's why I wrote this book.

I wanted to create a guide that would help shorten your learning curve, give you confidence, and encourage you to start building your own financial future with wisdom and intention.

My hope is that these pages have given you more than information. I hope they've given you belief. I hope they've helped you see that wealth isn't created overnight. Like any beautiful garden, it's built one seed, one season, and one faithful decision at a time.

The financial world will continue to evolve. Technology will continue to advance. New opportunities will continue to emerge. You don't need to know everything before you begin.

Just get started.

As I like to say, build the plane as you fly it.

If you'd like to continue this journey with me and have someone walking alongside you every step of the way, I'd love to welcome you into The Inner Circle.

The Inner Circle is where I share ongoing market education, digital asset updates, investment opportunities I'm researching, and the lessons I'm learning as this new financial era continues to unfold. More importantly, it's a community of like-minded people who are committed to growing together, asking questions, encouraging one another, and building lasting wealth with confidence.

Before you close this book, I also encourage you to spend a few minutes exploring the Resources section. I've included many of the websites, tools, books, communities, and educational resources that have helped shape my own investing journey. My hope is that they'll continue supporting you long after you've turned the final page.

I truly believe we're living through one of the greatest financial transformations of our lifetime, and I believe this is only the beginning.

Thank you for trusting me enough to spend these hours together. It has been an incredible honor to walk beside you, and I sincerely hope this book becomes one of the seeds that transforms your family's financial future for generations to come.

One day, I hope our paths cross. Please share your success with me!

I love to connect online, at a live event, inside The Inner Circle, or through a message telling me how this book changed your life, nothing would bring me more joy than hearing your story.

Until then...

Keep preparing.

Keep planting.

Keep protecting.

Keep prospering.

And never stop believing in the incredible future you're capable of creating.

I can't wait to see what you grow.

With Infinite Love & Prosperity,

Jenny Connolley

APPENDIX

Crypto Language Cheat Sheet

Beginner's Guide to Understanding Crypto Terms

💰 Investment Terms

DCA (Dollar Cost Averaging) – Investing a fixed amount of money at regular intervals, regardless of whether prices are rising or falling. This strategy helps smooth out market volatility over time.

ROI (Return on Investment) – The percentage gain or loss compared to your original investment.

ATH (All-Time High) – The highest price a cryptocurrency or asset has ever reached.

ATL (All-Time Low) – The lowest price a cryptocurrency or asset has ever reached.

MC (Market Cap) – The total value of a cryptocurrency, calculated by multiplying the current price by the number of coins in circulation.

Portfolio – The collection of all your investments.

Diversification – Spreading your investments across different assets to reduce risk.

Asset Allocation – How your investments are divided between different asset types.

Passive Income – Income earned from investments with minimal ongoing effort.

Compounding – Earning returns on both your original investment and previous gains.

Capital Gain – The profit made when you sell an investment for more than you paid.

Capital Loss – The loss incurred when you sell an investment for less than you paid.

Trading Language

HODL (Hold On for Dear Life) – Holding your cryptocurrency for the long term despite market volatility.

FOMO (Fear Of Missing Out) – Buying because prices are rising and you fear missing an opportunity.

FUD (Fear, Uncertainty and Doubt) – Negative news, rumors, or sentiment that creates fear among investors.

TP (Take Profit) – Selling part of your investment after it has increased in value to lock in profits.

SL (Stop Loss) – A preset price where an investment is automatically sold to limit losses.

BTFD (Buy The Dip) – Buying an asset after its price has fallen, believing it will recover over time.

Pump – A rapid increase in price.

Dump – A rapid decline in price.

Dip – A temporary fall in price.

Correction – A healthy pullback in price after a significant rise.

Support – A price level where buyers tend to step in, preventing further declines.

Resistance – A price level where selling pressure often prevents prices from rising higher.

Trading Pair – Two assets that can be traded against each other, such as BTC/USD or ETH/BTC.

Spread – The difference between the buying and selling price.

Volume – The total amount of an asset traded over a given period.

🧠 Crypto Mindset Terms

Bull Market – A period where prices are generally rising.

Bear Market – A period where prices are generally falling.

Bullish – Expecting prices to rise.

Bearish – Expecting prices to fall.

Volatility – Rapid price movements in either direction.

Liquidity – How easily an asset can be bought or sold.

Conviction – Confidence in your investment despite short-term market movements.

Market Sentiment – The overall mood or attitude of investors.

Long-Term Investor – Someone who invests with a long-term outlook rather than reacting to daily price movements.

Diamond Hands – Holding investments confidently through market ups and downs.

Paper Hands – Selling investments too quickly because of fear.

Whale – An individual or institution that owns a very large amount of cryptocurrency.

Retail Investor – An everyday individual investor.

Institutional Investor – Large organizations such as banks, hedge funds, or investment firms.

Wallet & Security Terms

Wallet – A digital wallet used to store and manage cryptocurrency.

Hot Wallet – A wallet connected to the internet for convenient access.

Cold Wallet – A wallet stored offline for maximum security.

Hardware Wallet – A physical device that securely stores cryptocurrency offline.

Software Wallet – A wallet installed on your computer or smartphone.

Private Key – A secret code that proves ownership of your cryptocurrency.

Public Address – The address you share with others so they can send you cryptocurrency.

Seed Phrase – A list of recovery words used to restore access to your wallet. Never share it with anyone.

2FA (Two-Factor Authentication) – An additional layer of security that requires a second verification step.

KYC (Know Your Customer) – Identity verification required by many cryptocurrency exchanges.

AML (Anti-Money Laundering) – Regulations designed to prevent financial crime.

Phishing – A scam that tricks people into revealing passwords or seed phrases.

Scam Token – A fake or fraudulent cryptocurrency designed to deceive investors.

Rug Pull – A scam where developers abandon a project after taking investors' money.

🌐 Blockchain Terms

Blockchain – A secure, transparent digital ledger that records every transaction.

Bitcoin (BTC) – The world's first and largest cryptocurrency.

Altcoin – Any cryptocurrency other than Bitcoin.

Coin – A cryptocurrency that operates on its own blockchain.

Token – A cryptocurrency built on an existing blockchain.

Stablecoin – A cryptocurrency designed to maintain a stable value by being linked to a traditional currency.

Block – A collection of verified transactions added to the blockchain.

Node – A computer that helps verify and secure blockchain transactions.

Mining – The process of validating transactions and creating new coins on certain blockchains.

Miner – A computer or participant that validates blockchain transactions.

Staking – Locking cryptocurrency to help secure a blockchain while earning rewards.

Validator – A participant who verifies blockchain transactions.

Hash – A unique digital fingerprint used to secure blockchain data.

Gas Fee – The fee paid to process transactions on a blockchain.

Smart Contract – A self-executing digital agreement that automatically carries out programmed instructions.

Layer 1 – A primary blockchain such as Bitcoin, Ethereum, Solana, or Cardano.

Layer 2 – Technology built on top of a blockchain to improve speed and reduce transaction costs.

🌍 Crypto Ecosystem

DeFi (Decentralized Finance) – Financial services that operate without traditional banks.

NFT (Non-Fungible Token) – A unique digital asset representing ownership of an item or collectible.

DAO (Decentralized Autonomous Organization) – A community-led organization governed through blockchain voting.

DEX (Decentralized Exchange) – A platform where users trade cryptocurrency directly with one another.

CEX (Centralized Exchange) – A company that facilitates buying, selling, and storing cryptocurrency.

Tokenomics – The economic design of a cryptocurrency, including supply, demand, and utility.

Utility – The real-world purpose of a cryptocurrency.

Whitepaper – A project's official document explaining its technology, purpose, and goals.

Roadmap – A project's planned future developments.

Use Case – The real-world problem a cryptocurrency or blockchain project aims to solve.

Adoption – The increasing use of cryptocurrency by individuals, businesses, and institutions.

Consensus – The process used by a blockchain network to agree that transactions are valid.

🚀 Popular Crypto Sayings

DYOR (Do Your Own Research) – Always research thoroughly before investing.

WAGMI (We're All Gonna Make It) – A phrase expressing optimism within the crypto community.

NGMI (Not Gonna Make It) – A humorous phrase used when someone repeatedly makes poor investment decisions.

LFG (Let's Freaking Go!) – An expression of excitement and enthusiasm.

GM (Good Morning) – A common greeting within the crypto community that promotes positivity.

To The Moon – A belief that a cryptocurrency's price will rise dramatically.

Bag Holder – Someone still holding an investment after its value has dropped significantly.

Ape In – Investing quickly without doing adequate research.

Shill – Promoting a cryptocurrency enthusiastically, sometimes for personal gain.

REKT – Crypto slang for suffering a significant financial loss.

Honeypot – A scam where investors can buy a token but cannot sell it.

Meme Coin – A cryptocurrency inspired by internet memes or popular culture, often driven by community enthusiasm rather than utility.

RESOURCES

To access all of the resources mentioned throughout this book, visit:

JennyConnolley.com/GoldenGardenBlueprint

You'll find everything gathered in one place, kept current, and ready for you to use:

- **The Inner Circle** — join the community and keep growing alongside others
- **My Mentor's OUTSTANDING Group** — details on the group where my own roots began
- **How to Buy Crypto** — choosing an exchange, setting up your account, and securing your wallet
- **Discover Your Soul Blueprint** — book a private Vedic Astrology Reading to uncover your gifts, life purpose, and timing
- **Financial Garden Worksheet** — build a clear picture of where you stand today
- **Design Your Confidence Resume** — created with Molly Smith

Scan the QR code below to visit the book resources page:

About the Author

Jenny Connolley is an investor, educator, entrepreneur, and Intuitive Wealth Mentor dedicated to helping people build extraordinary wealth from the inside out. She knows true prosperity begins long before a dollar is invested. It begins by healing scarcity, expanding identity, and learning to steward every gift, opportunity, and resource with wisdom and purpose.

With a finance degree and more than 25 years of investing experience, Jenny has spent her career studying wealth creation, financial psychology, and the principles that separate those who simply earn money from those who create lasting financial freedom. She has been actively investing in digital assets since 2017, researching emerging technologies and the evolution of the global financial system while helping others develop the confidence to become long-term investors.

Before dedicating her life to financial education, Jenny built and sold a multimillion-dollar roofing company, proving firsthand that wealth is created through vision, resilience, discipline, and consistent action. Her entrepreneurial journey has taken her through both incredible success and profound personal challenges, giving her a unique perspective on what it truly means to build a life of significance.

Jenny's work extends far beyond finances. She is a Master NLP Practitioner, certified life coach, breathwork facilitator, and transformational mentor who has devoted years to understanding the connection between mindset, emotional healing, nervous system regulation, and financial behavior. She believes that lasting wealth isn't created by information alone. It is created when knowledge and identity come together.

After experiencing the sudden loss of both parents, navigating seasons of grief, rebuilding her life, and choosing a path of healing and sobriety, Jenny discovered that the greatest transformations begin within. Those experiences reshaped her definition of wealth. Today, she teaches that real prosperity includes peace, health, meaningful relationships, purpose, generosity, and financial abundance working together.

As the founder of Intuitive Wealth Academy and The Inner Circle, Jenny is passionate about making financial education approachable, especially for women who feel behind on retirement, intimidated by investing, or uncertain where to begin. Her mission is to simplify complex financial concepts, inspire confident action, and empower people to participate in what she is very confident is the greatest wealth-building opportunities of this generation through education, stewardship, and long-term thinking.

Jenny's vision reaches far beyond personal financial success. She believes wealth is a responsibility as much as it is a blessing. Her life's mission is to help create a generation of intuitive wealth stewards—people who use their prosperity to strengthen families, uplift communities, support meaningful causes, and leave the world better than they found it. She often says that legacy is not measured by what we accumulate, but by the lives we impact through faithful stewardship.

When she isn't teaching, writing, or mentoring, Jenny enjoys spending time with her husband, Tom, and their beloved horses in Florida, where many of her greatest ideas are born in the quiet rhythm of nature. Through her books, courses, community, and speaking, she continues to inspire people around the world to dream bigger, steward wisely, and create a future filled with freedom, purpose, generosity, and lasting abundance.

To learn more, visit **JennyConnolley.com** and join the growing community of individuals committed to building wealth that creates a better world.

www.ingramcontent.com/pod-product-compliance
Lightning Source LLC
LaVergne TN
LVHW052315200926
848481LV00002B/568